This book is dedicated to my Aunt Carol, our family's angel.
You were my first mentor, safe harbor in stormy weather,
and always my true North Star.
Thank you for loving me so much.

Contents

Contents

Part 2   What the Best Do Better than Anyone Else

Contents

Part 3   Perfect Phrases That Activate Employee Development Plans

Contents

Preface

*A*merica's got talent in the workplace—and it comes from all over the world! This is the premise for this, my second *Perfect Phrases* book—the first was *Perfect Phrases for Documenting Employee Performance Problems*—and now you hold in your hands *Perfect Phrases for Employee Development Plans*. Later in this book I will address the powerful ways and strategic methods behind my approach. It's all about developing creative and practical employee development plans, and it will provide you with lots of lists and phrases to help you piece together your own employee development scenarios, useful for employees at every level within the organization.

When I was asked to author another book in this powerful management series on employee development plans, the timing could not have been better. I was smack in the middle of rolling out my 2010–2011 training series and launching a new website. I had just finished working alongside and interviewing leaders in top organizations from all over the world on the various ways and perfect phrases they use to develop and grow talent in the workplace.

As a result, I have included in this book a wide variety of multicultural and multigenerational phrases, lists, questions, and managerial advice that you will be able to refer to again and again as you formulate your own employee development plans.

Bozeman to Budapest

America's talent comes from all corners of the planet, and I wrote this book to share with you global approaches and methods that will not only help you build stronger employee development plans but will help you get others to work together more synergistically. Even if you're a virtual manager who is responsible for developing talent from a distance—from Denver to Dubai—this book can help.

This book contains hundreds of phrases you are sure to benefit from. Many of them have proven helpful to me, repeatedly. It's my hope that you will find yourself using and applying these phrases, tips, tools, and techniques to better adopt, modify, or expand your employee development plans so that you can more easily meet your specific organizational needs and people development requirements. This user-friendly guide will be a constant companion for you and other managers and leaders as you navigate the delicate process of creating each individual employee development plan.

What's Missing from Traditional HR Practices and Career Counseling

I have been immersed in the development of human talent for almost 20 years now, mostly through my keynote speaking, consulting, and training engagements worldwide, and I'm here to tell you there has been an enormous shift in how managers and leaders are approaching this particular subject in the 21st century.

We can no longer rely on the same old traditional HR practices, career counseling, or business-as-usual career guidance we once used. In today's breakneck-speed world of employee development, it's important that we stay current and do our best to keep up with cutting-edge people practices, and those practices are not at all what they used to be, or what you may have learned about in a Management 101 class.

Most likely this book will give you a glimpse at areas you've yet to study or practice on the job when it comes to day-to-day people development and business practices. It's now business as *un*usual, as I like to call it. In other words, employee development, or growing employees over time, and the plans that support the overall effort to do this successfully are not your grandfather's or even your mother's Oldsmobile anymore! People development is moving at Mach 1 speed. It's all about growing better, stronger, upgradable, and more capable and self-reliant talent that will take your organization into the future. More than technology, this, in my opinion, is the critical issue of the decade. So buckle up!

Employee development worldwide is taking a whole new twist and numerous turns, and it's time to shake the old methods of employee development and adopt some of the new and exciting ways to grow talent in your organization for the future survival of your business and the well-being of every single person, on each and every team. As Dr. Maya Angelou says, "Now that we know better, we must do better." This book is definitely a step in the right direction toward doing better when it comes to creating dynamic employee development plans and helping to facilitate the success of each person moving forward on his or her own career path.

Three Key Changes in Employee Development Plans

This book contains hundreds of phrases that have grown organically from the three primary changes we, as managers, must be aware of when it comes to growing our people and developing talent. These changes require that we

- Stop focusing on people's weaknesses and start focusing on developing their strengths
- Start minding the gaps in employee performance by neutralizing, not "fixing," each person's struggles, challenges, and perceived weaknesses. To neutralize means to "defuse" an employee's challenges and weak areas that managers tend to focus on and feel driven to improve regardless of a person's competency to do so. When we neutralize a person's weaknesses, we "equalize" the playing field of talent and shift efforts more organically and naturally to inflating strengths. When this happens, a manager can actually feel the struggles his or her employee might be experiencing start to decompress. Magnification of the employee's weakness shifts to finding a more comfortable way to create basic competency for the task and allow the employee's natural talent to take over.

■ Provide practical and realistic employee development plans that grow and develop talent not only professionally but on a personal level as well

Harness the Power

It's time to harness the power of employee development plans, and this book will help you to do it. This book is a powerful communication tool for managers and leaders everywhere—a fast, easy-to-reference, real-world field guide to making positive behavioral advances in the workplace through effective employee development planning. Managers today are faced with higher performance requirements, with less time to make it all happen. Superfast and practical is the mantra, and ready references like the ones in this book for supervisors and managers at all levels serve as much-needed and appreciated survival tools.

If you're a manager who wants to more effectively grow talent and create impressive employee development plans, then this book is for you. It offers reader-friendly tips and tools that I have gathered over the years working with the finest managers and leaders from some of the world's top organizations. You will find that all of these techniques help promote individual growth and learning, as well as personal and professional development in a 21st-century workplace filled with tough challenges.

We work in a time when employee growth and talent development issues are often unique, potentially exhausting, and more challenging than ever for today's manager. How you choose to equip yourself to keep moving forward and handle these challenges is what will separate you from the herd and move you and your employees forward in a positive and evolving direction.

Exceptional employee development plans, the kind that truly make a difference, always come down to two things: movement and momentum. I'm confident that this book will provide you with both for an exciting and successful outcome to each and every employee development plan you build.

The journey has just begun. I'm glad we're making it together.

Acknowledgments

There are some things I never thought I'd see in my lifetime:

- Paul McCartney remarrying and divorcing
- An 85-year-old couple going through a security checkpoint in the airport on their 60th wedding anniversary and getting stripped of their shoes, metal canes, and denture cream to ensure they weren't going to explode!
- Prices of $5 for an eight-ounce bottle of water and $6 for a cup of coffee
- And, most surprising, the release of this, my 14th book!

None of these books would have been possible if the audiences I speak to and train for did not quickly go to their BlackBerrys or laptops and start placing book orders with Amazon.com and other booksellers—sometimes before I even leave the stage.

Thank you to every person who has at one time or another attended one of my seminars, training events, workshops, or keynote speeches. And to all of you who keep coming back, bringing friends, and buying my books—without your support, there would not be this book. Just know that the heartfelt stories you share with me and your personal e-mails, letters, cards, and helpful feedback continue to enrich my life by allowing me to remain a part of yours. I'm truly honored.

Next, I have two families to thank—the one I am related to by blood and friendship and the one I am related to via the publishing world. McGraw-Hill has been my publishing family for 15 years. To my editor Brian Foster—it is my first time working with you, and it's been a pleasure every step of the way. What people don't see in this book is your consummate professionalism, mindful guidance, and easy-to-get-along-with nature. You tolerated my numerous phone messages and weird sense of humor when I was bone tired from flying from one airport to another. For that alone, you get big points!

To the awesome and talented team of editors and production staff at McGraw-Hill Publishing, including assistant project editor Joseph Berkowitz, EDP supervisor Craig Bolt, copyeditor Allison Shurtz, and so many others in sales and marketing, publicity, and graphic arts—you are truly the unsung heroes of the publishing world. You make the hard work and behind-the-scenes efforts of creating books appear seamless. Thank you all for working your magic on this book.

If there were a book called *Perfect Friends and Family*, I'd be the author. You cannot write books for a living and fly more than 100,000 miles a year speaking on the subjects of those books if you don't have the unconditional support and love from friends and family. I cannot list everyone, but you know who you are: thank you from the bottom of my heart.

Acknowledgments

During the writing of this book, I had some very dedicated people come to my aid and stand by me when I was spinning many plates and trying not to drop any of them. You are the ones who got me through the deadlines of this year's projects, and I'd like to acknowledge you here.

Thank you to the amazingly talented Jonathan Halls, of Jonathan Halls and Associates, for shooting video of me at the ASTD (American Society for Training and Development) conference, hanging out all day shooting even more video for my new website, then editing it all with lightning speed. You've been a great friend, and your helpfulness and advice have been invaluable. Thank you *mompreneur* and superfast editor Phyllis Salamone Jask for your friendship and many insights on my last two book projects. And thanks to Vinny and baby Robin for your cooperation too. For all the late-night, marathon telephone calls, always sharing with me your never-ending support and wisdom, a big thank-you goes to Betty Garrett—agent, angel, and forever-friend. To my adopted brothers Lawrence Polsky and Antoine Gerschel, for all the flowers, candy, and nonstop friendship and support—especially during those final deadline days—a million thank-yous! To Anmarie Miller, a big hug to you for all you do for me. You have a heart bigger than the great state of Texas.

For Elly Mixsell, aka AnneBruce.com website fashionista, we've been working together now for 15 years, and what an unbeatable team we make. You continue to take all that I do on my website, and in my training workbooks, and make it so much better than I could have imagined. Thanks for letting me be Victoria and Catherine's Godmommy and for being such a treasured friend. To the mighty Team Attitude: Sam Glenn,

Acknowledgments

Jocelyn Godfrey, and Michelle Arnold, my deepest appreciation for your support of my work and your amazing friendship—you all rock! To Kim Lehner, I'm so grateful for and deeply cherish our 40-year friendship. You have always been there for me, unconditionally, through sunshine and rain. To Traci Van and Casey, you are my favorite cheerleaders and always lift me up, up, up! Love you both! To the dynamic duo, Debbie and Mark Berg—you inspire me to be a better person every day. And to Glenda Thomas and Diane Panvelle, you will never know how extraordinary I think you both are.

To my sister Rose Marie Trammell for always being there; my cousins Theresa (best friends are we, my cousin and me) and Bob Kautz, Anthony and Dolores Cassini; to dearest friends and gator pals Carole and Harris Herman; Sherry Hancock, for your beautiful cards, Paris memory book, and special notes on exquisite stationery; fellow superstar speaker and Denver gal pal Julie Wassom; brilliant goddaughter and the "next" Mary Roach of science writing, Katie McKissick; supersweet sister-in-law Helen Ireland; my beautiful nieces Kathleen Wolsfeld and Ashley Trammell; BFF since we were 12, *MyTable* publisher and editor extraordinaire Teresa Byrne-Dodge; media maven Dee Damron Monroe; and dearest and devoted friends Wilson Smith, Maureen McKissick, Debbie Dolenga, Stephanie Dolenga, and Jennifer Seifert—no author could ask for a more amazing cheering gallery.

And finally, to the light that inspires me to shine in all that I do—my daughter Autumn Kelly Mostovoj. Thank you for always believing in me. I am so proud of the beautiful and brilliant woman you are, both inside and out. And to my son-in-law, firefighter Andy Mostovoj, a big thank-you for your continuous

Acknowledgments

words of encouragement and bravery. And especially to my husband, David, who encourages me to be more than I could ever dream possible. Thanks for being the hearth-hugger when I am off on the road and for reheating the spaghetti for dinner!

Introduction

*E*mployee development and skydiving are very much the same—both require enormous trust and taking a leap of faith. As managers, we teach what we know, and we often use the tools we feel comfortable with and have relied on time and again. And that's okay, to a point. It's only human to want to ensure the success of our efforts and the efforts of the people we are training and developing. Our employees' ultimate success (or safe landing, to use the skydiving metaphor) is a reflection on how well we've developed their potential and talent up to that point.

How many times have you coached or trained an employee using some of the old-school methods that you relied on back in the day? The approach may not be right or wrong, good or bad. It's just human nature that we sometimes instill in others what we know to be best for us, rather than what may be best for them at the time. One of the action learning points I teach in my seminars and workshops states, "We cannot coach people down a path that is inconsistent with the way that they see themselves." Our employees may eventually grow beyond anything we could have imagined for them, and we may never know where our influence stops.

So we may start off using our own methods and what worked best for us at one time, but eventually, to be able to develop people to their greater level of potential and performance, we have to relinquish our power and let them take the lead. I write about this extensively in my book *Be Your Own Mentor*, published by McGraw-Hill. It is our job to facilitate the success of others. It is the employees' responsibility to be their own mentor and make things happen in their own way and with their own flair and style. We make the journey together, and sometimes it starts at a skydiving drop zone.

As I said, employee development planning is similar to skydiving with a coach, and I've done both. Each requires enormous leaps of faith from both parties involved. In this metaphor, *the employee is the skydiving student, the manager is the skydiving instructor, and the parachute is the employee development plan.* How pretty the parachute is, or what color it is, means nothing if the parachute doesn't open and function for a safe adventure, with a smooth landing at the end. Employee development plans, like parachutes, have to be sturdy, substantive, reliable, strong, flexible, real-world based, user-friendly, easy to navigate and manipulate, and able to steer to the ultimate career drop zone.

Your ultimate objective is to provide each and every employee with the best tools and resources available to help ensure a successful journey and safe landing. Once you've provided the map and compass, it's time for both you and your employee to take the ultimate leap of faith and implement the plan.

What Is an Employee Development Plan?

Employees are hardwired for success—provided they have a plan. An employee development plan is a written strategy that provides the employee with a step-by-step process that will help the person to achieve his or her career goals. The plan's purpose is to develop the employee's strengths to his or her greatest levels of talent and competency, achievement, and greater potential. An employee development plan is also called a career development plan, individual development plan, or career-pathing strategy.

Employee development plans include the perspectives of both a supervisor or manager and his or her employee. The goal is to make the plan reasonable and attainable, something that the employee can achieve with dedication, hard work, and focus. It's your job as a manager or supervisor to set every employee up for success, not failure. We set people up for success when we let them shine at what they are good at, work at what they love doing, and continue to build a track record of success around those competencies.

Focusing on Employee Weaknesses Will Backfire on a Manager

The most beneficial employee development plan focuses on an employee's talents and strengths. It does not shine the light solely, or focus solely, on the person's weaknesses and how to improve them. Weak areas and challenges are certainly discussed and covered, but they are not, nor should they ever be, the primary focus for growing talent in an organization. The plan will backfire if you do.

Weaknesses and special challenge areas of every employee should be discussed and then neutralized in an individual development plan, thereby making way for and allowing the employee's greatest talents to be fueled. Neutralizing weaknesses requires that you give the employee the help he or she needs to be able to do the job to the required competency level, but not necessarily exceed that level. You don't want to spend an inordinate amount of time focusing on someone's weaknesses. And you certainly don't want to spend an inordinate amount of time pushing someone down a path that he or she hates or developing a skill set that the person despises doing—even if he or she is capable of pulling it off. The results will be disastrous not only for the employee, but also for the organization.

It's similar to when you were a kid in school. If you brought home a report card with four As, a B+, and one D−, chances are good your teacher and your parents spent one minute praising your As and Bs, but primarily focused on the D−. Sure that D− needed to be improved, but not necessarily to an A+ level of competency.

By only focusing on the weakness of the person, we make that person even weaker and more insecure. When we neutralize weaknesses and redirect our energy toward a person's strongest gifts and talents, we create superstar performers, confident men and women, and extraordinary contributors to the organization's long-term goals.

By identifying and fueling a person's strengths and strong suits, you better equip him or her for growth and success, and therefore, the organization as well. You acknowledge that these areas are what he or she is hardwired for. The organization and the employee come together to create a career plan that works in conjunction and is in alignment with the organization's mission and vision as well as the individual's desires and intrinsic motivation.

Check out the following employee phrases that tell managers what a person loves doing.

Employee Phrases That Say, "This Is What I Love Doing!"

- I can't wait to make my presentation on Tuesday.
- I love writing strategic plans for our team.
- I'd like to write a book someday.
- I read that publication regularly and enjoy it a lot.
- I'm good at planning events; call on me if you need my help.
- I love going to school and consider myself a lifelong learner.
- I'd like to start a book club in our department.
- This is so enjoyable—when can we do this again?
- I look forward to coming to work every day—I jump out of bed!
- I cannot believe how fast the time goes when I am working on this project.
- I'd do this job seven days a week if I could.
- It's exhilarating to volunteer.

- I love giving back to our community.
- I'm a people person.
- Music is in my soul—it inspires me to work harder.
- I'd like to coordinate a summer concert here on campus.
- I enjoy pushing myself and stretching my abilities to new heights.
- I look forward to stepping out of my comfort zone; it's scary, but I love it.
- I'd like to get politically active and make a real difference.
- I'm motivated by incentive plans and want to win that prize.
- I have a competitive nature and enjoy contests.
- The result of a job well done is very motivating to me.
- I love learning the newest technology and then using it on the job.
- I'm pretty talented at that.
- That's one of my strong suits; I'd like to help.
- I love a good challenge—let's do it.
- I'm not afraid of risks; in fact, I consider myself quite a risk taker.
- Nothing ventured, nothing gained.
- I'm in the science club, and that's how I spend my Saturdays.
- This is the most fun I've ever had!
- There's nothing like flying your own plane!
- I'd do this all day, every day, without getting paid!
- I live for sports!

- I had no idea how thrilling this would be.

- This never bores me.

- I feel alive when I'm doing this.

- I'll bring a dish to the potluck; I love cooking.

- I'm the best party hostess—we can have the barbecue at my place.

- I want to travel everywhere and see the world any way possible.

- I'll take photographs for the company e-letter—I'm an amateur photographer and love taking pictures.

- I enjoy experimenting and trying out new things.

- I feel strong and confident every time I _____ .

- It's the best feeling when _____ .

- I've had some success at that; I'd like to give it a try.

- This really fulfills a great need of mine.

- I instinctively find myself looking forward to finding solutions and figuring out puzzles.

- I can concentrate on these things easily. They get my synapses firing like mad!

- I'm in the zone when I am doing this.

- I'm introverted, so I love quiet time alone to think and plan ahead.

- I could make this a full-time hobby.

- My areas of strength make me feel like I'm growing.

- Self-development helps me to reach my higher potential.

- When I am coaching others, I am learning the most.

- I have the patience for this when most do not.

- I yearn for success and achievement.
- I use a vision board to set my goals.
- I love being on a team!
- I enjoy motivating others and infusing the can-do spirit into the team.
- I have both a personal and a professional mission statement I take seriously.
- I have something special to offer in this area and want to apply myself here.
- I want to keep sharpening the saw in this skill set.
- I know what I'm good at, and that makes me feel confident.
- I like being hands-on.
- If it's fun, I can do anything.
- Doing this really makes me happy.
- Being here really makes me happy.
- I was born for this job.
- I never give up when it comes to this kind of project.
- I'm passionate about _____ .

Long-Term and Short-Term Goals

An employee development plan lists both short- and long-term goals that an employee has pertaining to the current and future opportunities available in the organization.

Perfect phrases for describing an employee's long-term and short-term goals within the company include:

- Wants to finish certification in a new area
- Desires to be selected for the next project management team in her division
- Studies through distance learning to improve skill sets
- Has set milestones in order to get promoted in two years
- Can express specific expectations
- Can express specific dislikes
- Checks in often with his or her supervisor to update on progress
- Documents what works and what doesn't
- Keeps lists of goals
- Asks questions regarding future opportunities and how he or she might fit into the picture
- Expresses realistic expectations
- Wants to know if there's time to develop skills he or she lacks
- Asks if there is anything different he or she can do to prepare for advancement
- Asks others to describe his or her strengths and weaknesses
- Always solicits honest feedback

- Wants advice on what kind of additional training to sign up for
- Wants to know about the career ladder in this organization
- Requests a coach for something specific
- Takes initiative toward all self-development opportunities
- Is prepared to use personal time and personal funds if necessary
- Considers external training an option
- Utilizes community activities as learning opportunities

What Is the Purpose of Having an Employee Development Plan?

The purpose of having an employee development plan (sometimes called an individual development plan, or IDP) is to grow talent and employee strengths within your organization. It has nothing to do with employee retention, or anyone paying you back, or appreciating what you've done for him or her, by staying employed at the organization for 30 years! That's not the way it works. As Zig Ziglar says, "If you help enough other people get everything they want in life, you will get everything you want and more." This applies to employee development plans as well.

If you help an employee plan a career strategy that is enormously successful and he or she chooses to leave your organization, then so be it. As I suggest to you later in this book, practice the FIDO principle: Forget it and drive on!

Regardless of where an employee winds up—retiring from your organization after many years or accepting a fantastic job offer with another organization, perhaps one you could not match—your intentions for him or her need to be pure and intended for the individual's growth and success. Whether you want to believe it or not, what goes around always comes around when it relates to business karma and to how we treat others and help prepare them for ongoing success and greater contribution. Your intentions have to be authentic and not self-serving. Employee development planning is a long-lasting and powerful tool. How you manage the responsibility is up to you.

Few people these days devote their entire work lives to one organization. Today's managers are well aware that if an employee (especially a younger employee) stays with an organization five or six years, that's a good run. Most Gen Xers and Gen Yers are not going to devote the next 30 years of their career life to any one organization. Yes, it can happen, but it's unlikely. That's not the way our fluid, faster-than-ever, virtual workplace is built anymore.

If you get the best someone has to offer for five or six years, then that's about all you can expect. If you get more than that, consider it a bonus—take it and be grateful for the loyalty and dedication. But remember, plenty of people out there (maybe you are one of them) are extremely grateful for the mentors they have had and the development they've received. It may just simply be time for the employee to move on for a wide variety of reasons. Have you ever moved on from someone or something? I bet you have. The key is in the relationship that we build along the way, not the people we hold hostage. Managers who continue to keep ongoing, strong personal and professional relationships with former employees find enormous benefit in the success that those they've mentored go on to achieve.

You're a manager and a leader, and leaders evolve. Teach others to do the same. You'll be glad you did in the end.

My advice to you reading this book: Learn to say good-bye, and mean it when you wish someone well.

An Easy Seven-Step Process for Employee Development Planning

The process for creating employee development plans can be whatever you want it to be. Experience tells us that a collaborative effort in designing a plan makes it stronger and more fluid. As the manager, you can guide the process and help to facilitate the success of the plan by collaborating with the individual on seven easy steps that examine the following key areas:

1. Competencies
2. Long-range goals
3. Short-range goals
4. Strategies
5. Action steps / timelines
6. Resources toolkit
7. Measurable outcomes

Getting Started

The process begins when you first sit down with an employee to identify big-picture goals, dreams, and objectives. Start out by having a relaxed and casual conversation about the employee's unique interests and talents. Inquire about his or her current position and how things are going. Ask if the employee is interested in any special assignments, training courses, or ways to contribute to the department he or she works in. Write all of this down. It's a time to listen, not talk.

Inquire about the person's different goals and obligations. Show your concern about family, using common sense and sensitivity and inquiring about community interests, because these are things that affect employee development planning big-time. For example, a great position might be available at another location. So it may be timely to ask the person whether he or she might consider relocating to a different city or state. If the answer is yes, this could become a goal within the plan. If the answer is no, then the plan will take a different direction and reflect those limitations. In addition, the worker might share with you that right now would be a difficult time to move elsewhere, but in two years the timing would be good. Then you could add "relocating for a new position" into the long-range goal category of this person's plan.

Offer resources you know of that are available both inside and outside the organization. Consult an HR specialist for assistance in identifying additional resources or tools. As I mentioned earlier, managers often use their own career development as a reference point for guiding the development of others. We can all easily fall into this trap without even thinking. But what worked for you as a manager or supervisor back then might not be the best plan for the worker sitting across from you now.

Start the preparation of an employee development plan. Set up times to meet with the worker to assess progress and changes and help him or her revise the plan as you go along. Provide assessment resources so the employee can establish a baseline of competency and self-score himself or herself in areas in which he or she can grow and flourish.

Do not wait a year before meeting again with the employee or only use annual performance review time to go over this plan. This is a work in progress. It will require ongoing brief and lengthier meetings to breathe life into the document.

Figures 1.1 and 1.2 show a template you can modify and adapt to your specific needs and the needs of your employees.

Before you take the development leap with your employees, read on, and you will find tons of helpful phrases and tips in this book to ensure a safe landing.

Figure 1.1   Career Drop Zone

Employee Development / Talent Development Template and Phrases

Competencies	Long-Range Goals	Short-Range Goals
Determine hard skills and soft skills.	See the big picture.	What can you do today? Right now?
Stand up for your strengths and talents.	Determine future opportunities and part you would like to play.	What can you do this week?
I feel strong and amazing when:	Start acting the part now for what you hope to become later.	What can you do this month?
Admit your weaknesses:		What can you do at the end of one year?
I feel depleted and exhausted when:	What must be done long term?	(Be as specific as possible re: all of the above questions)
Assessments to identify talents and strengths	Degree, certifications, new skill sets to learn, foreign language, possible relocation	How will technology change your field and career in the next three years?
Match competencies and talents to career choices.	How many coaches will you require?	What will you do to prepare for the future?
Set up collaborative sessions, meetings, discussions.	Who will you ask to mentor you?	How much money will it take?
Start draft of plan.		How long will training last?
Agree to neutralize challenge areas and weaknesses.		
What training will be required?		
How will research be approached?		
Define milestones.		
Determine what motivates you to your highest level of peak performance.		

Strategies	Action Steps / Timelines	Resources Toolkit	Measurable Outcomes
List specific strategies for both long-term and short-term goals.	Specific actions to be taken	Everything and anything that helps you to learn and grow and understand at a higher level	What did you love the most about getting here?
Who will be on your team?	Contacts to be made	Use and train for future technology.	Compare assessments initially taken with your results now.
Who are the key players?	Revisions to plan, by when? Review plan with manager.	Use and train for human development skills.	Use self-scoring card for measuring improvement.
What will you ask them to do?	Revise again checklist of what's been completed.	Seek out advanced mentors and coaches from inside and outside of the organization.	What percentage of improvement would you assign to your growth and development?
What will be your methods for moving things forward?	Due date progress meetings		
How will your employee development plan become a strategic tool?	Rethink milestones and pace.		How has what you've done over time increased organizational productivity and performance? Be specific.
How will you turn your strengths and talents into strategic weapons for winning and accomplishing your mission?	Record and document all input you are getting.	Make a list of resources you need to move ahead, share with your manager.	What specific areas can you point to that you have changed and improved processes within for the better?
Explain how you will handle change and make change work to your advantage.	What works? How can you do more? What doesn't work? How can you eliminate it?		Ask for feedback in all areas, measure its effectiveness.
Adopt a can-do attitude, use attitude as a strategy to move you out of difficult moments to greater success.			

Figure 1.2 Add Your Own Perfect Phrases Within Each Box and Create a Better, Stronger Personal and Professional Life

Competencies	Long-Range Goals	Short-Range Goals

Strategies	Action Steps / Timelines	Resources Toolkit	Measurable Outcomes

Part 1

Perfect Phrases That Build Employee Development Plans

Be the Architect of Employee Development in Your Organization

According to Ralph Waldo Emerson, "Our chief want is someone who will inspire us to be what we know we can be." This quote is a most fitting way to begin this particular *Perfect Phrases* section. It is what employee development planning is all about. And guess what? That "someone" Emerson describes is you! Today's manager is charged with doing everything better, cheaper, and lightning-speed faster, while embracing change, sometimes on a minute-by-minute basis, constantly upgrading workplace performance and productivity, and developing myriad customized employee development plans for the most multigenerational, multicultural, and diverse workforce the world has ever known, all while always thinking outside the box (no, make that *blowing up the box*).

Seriously, the responsibilities and expectations placed on today's supervisors and management leaders can feel daunting at times. However, becoming a successful architect of your employees' development plans does not require that you wait for the perfect employee, or the perfect job opening for that employee. You don't have to be the perfect manager or supervisor. And you certainly don't have to wait for the perfect situation, because that moment, frankly, may never come. Employee development is a work in progress, ongoing, full of human flaws, and a never-ending process of continuous learning. It's your job to take control of all these moving parts by effectively using the following phrases to build your employee development plans as they gradually and intentionally converge.

23

Upgrade Yourself First Before You Attempt to Upgrade Others

Use this book to shift your own paradigms and preconceived notions about employee development plans and, more important, how you see yourself as the architect of those plans. It starts with you, the leader.

When was the last time you took stock of your own personal and professional development? Forget about the last time you upgraded your cell phone, iPad, BlackBerry, iPhone, laptop, iPod, or other mobile technologies—when was the last time you upgraded *you*? Have you recently read a book, taken a class, attended a management or leadership seminar, completed that degree? Remember, you have to walk the talk if you are going to set the standards for others.

You Are Not Just a Manager: Reframing Who You Are

Do not limit how you see your role as a manager by what title you may have been assigned at your hiring or what is currently printed on your business card. Do not consider your title and present responsibilities as simply being a supervisor or manager. That's myopic thinking. And if you're myopic in visualizing your own talents and abilities, then your people will learn to limit their talents and abilities as well. The goal and intention of this book is to go beyond that. That means reframing your own professional and personal improvement plan by redefining who you are and what you really do. Here's how:

■ **First, envision the bigger picture of employee development planning.** You are *facilitating* the success of those around you. It's not your job or responsibility to actually *develop* your employees—that's their job.

It is your job and responsibility, however, to facilitate the development of others, and the following list of perfect phrases will be one portfolio tool you'll rely on again and again during the facilitation process.

Instead of selling your staff on a "how I would do it" approach, let employees at every level emerge on their own and discover their own talents, interests, and competencies. Encourage and inspire people at every level within your organization to want to take part in building a personal and professional development plan that will take them to the next higher level in their careers and then let this book be the road map, or plan of action, you use to build plans your employees can easily follow and grow from. It's that simple.

This is your opportunity as a manager, supervisor, and leader to reinvent yourself as a *developer of extraordinary people, strength strategist, excavator of exceptional talent and potential, inspiration and motivation finder, navigator of employee development skills and principles, and the co-architect of extraordinary employee development plans!* Are you up for the challenge?

■ **Second, it's called talent development for a reason.** The word *development* implies growth, nurturing talent, growing good workers into superb workers, forward and upward movement, momentum, building on strengths, adapting to new environments, modifying our ways as managers to fit new and better approaches, changing with the times, and loving every minute of it!

The word *development* also implies we are not stagnant, stuck, or suffering from analysis paralysis. When we get stuck, we cannot develop anyone or anything. When we focus merely on employee retention and old-school ways of career counseling, we miss the big-picture opportunities to grow employees to their highest level of achievement and potential. We miss the target, and the target is talent and the employees' strengths that talent represents.

As a manager, supervisor, or leader in your organization, it is your responsibility to not only help identify the unique talent within every employee, at every level of the organization, but it's your job to nurture and support the development of every person's skill sets. This book will be your tool to do that successfully.

■ **Third, employee development, at every level, requires a plan of action.** It all starts with understanding and knowing what employee development and growing talent is all about, finding the lists of phrases specifically designed for every group you seek to develop, studying the examples of world-class organizations and their employee development plans, and finally, activating the various components of growing talent and employee strengths that help you to not only keep, but grow the strengths and neutralize the weaknesses of the people who keep your business in business!

Remember, employee retention is *not*, or should it ever be, the focus. Developing people is the focus, and the natural extension and outgrowth of that genuine effort will be employee loyalty and retention.

How to Apply and Tailor These Perfect Phrases

Consider your employees' skill levels. Ask yourself if the people you are developing are novices, masters, or somewhere in between. Tailor all employee development plans to the level of your employees' competencies. You wouldn't design the same plan for an entry-level worker that you would for a seasoned, experienced worker, would you? By doing so, you'd quickly squelch the confidence of the novice and de-motivate the more seasoned performer.

Assess Experience

Take time to assess how much experience your employees have in the specific area in which you are offering career counseling and development. A new hire may have learned the basic skills but may never have had a chance to use them on the job. Employees who have lots of real-world experience will bring a different dynamic to the personal and professional development process—they've been there, done that. The more experienced workers may also need to reignite their passion for their careers, especially if they have become somewhat jaded along the way, or complacent and too comfortable.

Keep Raising the Bar

Remember, employees who have honed their skills over time are often seeking a challenge in their careers. These people need to be fired up! As a leader you can use experienced employees' talents to your advantage. These are often your superstars. Don't let them become complacent or bored. Keep these top performers on their toes and use an employee development plan to challenge them to rise higher and stretch themselves. Employee development plans are often just the ticket to light an experienced worker's inner fire and to motivate him or her to take on bigger and more difficult challenges. If you don't try this approach, or just give up, the employee may quickly become de-motivated and possibly even tune you out, if it hasn't happened already.

The following perfect phrases take all of these issues into consideration. They are organized in lists that apply to each separate group described. Keep in mind that no one knows the needs of the organization or the needs of the people better than you do as one of its leaders. So select the perfect phrases that best match those needs to build employee development plans that put all of your employees' strengths to work.

Formula for Success: Adapt, Delete, Modify, and Expand

Adapt, delete, modify, and expand the following phrases, statements, and questions to best meet your objectives and the needs of your people. Invite your employees to help you do this. Give your employees the opportunity to help write their own personal and professional development plans. You'll be glad you did.

Perfect Phrases for Interns and Temps

- Knows what motivates him or her early on and is willing to share with supervisor and manager
- Offers fresh ideas and new ways of looking at situations
- Prepares in advance to impress leadership
- Realizes this is the beginning but is already preparing for a leadership role
- Takes on first position with confidence and willingness to learn
- Stays clear of pitfalls from organizational politics and employee conflict
- Gets noticed by acting in a mature and responsible way
- Quickly learns to adapt his or her style to the styles of others and what is acceptable within the team, yet still maintains individuality of thought and contribution
- Observes how others succeed at getting buy-in and support from others
- Is always preparing to take the next step
- Accepts that there is much to learn
- Knows this isn't a time for answers but a time to ask smart questions
- Describes with clarity his or her future interests and ambitions
- Demonstrates curiosity and wants to explore various interests
- Wants to help create a plan with supervisor that piques other employees' interest about future possibilities or new projects for the team

- Ties interests outside the workplace into professional goals
- Seeks opportunities to familiarize himself or herself with the organization
- Seeks out a workplace mentor or coach
- Pursues continuing education via on-the-job training and professional organizations in his or her field
- Networks with others in the organization who do what he or she does
- Networks with others in the organization who do something different
- Networks with others in the same field from different organizations
- Is comfortable learning new things
- Is willing to take on new tasks and responsibilities
- Embraces new technology with confidence—gets really excited about it!
- Welcomes new learning opportunities with enthusiasm and gusto
- Enjoys learning from others
- Is excited to be on board and shows it
- Understands the organization's purpose and is eager to describe his or her part in making it happen
- Uses the organization's equipment responsibly and asks for help when necessary
- Has a strong work ethic and can describe his or her core values
- Is punctual and considerate of others' time

- Comes to work on time and is rarely absent
- Consistently demonstrates a good attitude
- Takes care of himself or herself, is accountable
- Wears appropriate clothing for the task at hand—in the field with linemen—for example, wears steel-toe boots and helmet, jeans, and T-shirt
- Uses appropriate language and grammar, doesn't mumble
- Takes responsibility for work
- Owns up to mistakes
- Is honest and sincere
- Contributes with pride to the success of the organization
- Accepts feedback responsibly and appropriately; says, "Thanks for your feedback."
- Communicates effectively with both peers and managers
- Stretches himself or herself to reach a higher bar, likes the challenge
- Shows appreciation and common courtesies; is very polite
- Confident, yet realizes there's a lot to learn and get answers to, has a good reality check system in place

Perfect Phrases for Recent College Grads

- Looks forward to having this first job tie into his or her strengths and interest
- Seeks to connect higher learning to higher performance on the job
- Links academic experiences to real-world, on-the-job solutions
- Sees his or her employee development as a natural extension of four years in college—a similar, deliberate plan to succeed on the job
- Reconnects with college adviser or career counselor for advice and guidance on starting a first job
- Asks friends and family for any contacts they might know in the same field of work who might provide solid career advice and resources
- Researches all aspects of the organization, its history, and its culture
- Reads press clippings and researches media archives on the organization and its people
- Can describe, "What I like doing and talents I've had since I was a kid"
- Talks about favorite subjects in school and professors who taught them
- Can complete the following statement with confidence: "_____ is what I do best, and I feel great when I do it."
- Has a strong desire to continue his or her education throughout his or her career with higher degrees, certificate programs, employee training, seminars, distance learning, e-learning, webinars, teleseminars, and so on

- Excited about the use of helpful technology throughout his or her education and now in his or her career and the future
- Blends e-mailing, IMing, texting, tweeting, Facebooking, and all the latest services available
- Is mature
- Maintains a professional, but not dated, appearance; fits the current business casual image
- Participates in workplace fun and seeks higher productivity and performance levels through effective behavior and communication skills
- Dresses in alignment with the organization's culture—at Southwest Airlines, it's shorts and a polo shirt; on Wall Street, it's a suit, a starched shirt, and dress shoes
- Has good personal hygiene—clean, put together, comfortable, fresh
- Uses appropriate language and grammar
- When stressing a point, communicates without profanity
- Tells the world who he or she is with strong written communication skills; uses good grammar, not abbreviations, emoticons, or textspeak
- Wants to give back, joins professional associations, volunteers
- Easily meets others with similar career interests
- Applies school lessons to real-world scenarios
- Recognizes that bad habits don't improve with age
- Manages "instant gratification" needs with ongoing employee development

- Implements strengths and uses knowledge of technologies to grow skill sets
- Welcomes learning opportunities from other cultures and levels within the organization
- Uses good judgment and practices commonsense decision making
- Understands the purpose of the organization and outcomes of the project
- Knows when to seek assistance, is not afraid to ask questions
- Offers advice on how to recruit other college talent
- Starts out developing good listening skills
- Sees observation as a key learning tool
- Focuses, is not easily distracted or taken off task by little things
- Completes assignments by deadline
- Accepts that older generations can provide invaluable tools and real-world experience to be learned from and collaborated with
- Feels confident in teaching more experienced workers things they may not know about technology or more trendy workplace issues
- Consistently looks to be in alignment with the bigger picture and goals of the organization and its leadership
- Maintains contact with college professors for ongoing advice during transition from college to the workplace
- Alignment with industry and formal career plan attained through a higher-level degree (master's, MBA, or Ph.D.)

Perfect Phrases for Boomers, Seniors, and Seasoned Vets (50s to Upper 60s)

- Learns from others across age, gender, and culture lines
- Seeks to find commonality
- Treats everyone with respect
- Embraces new ways of doing things
- Old dogs learn new tricks, new dogs learn from old dogs
- Has learned to blend, not just balance, work and home life
- Embraces new technologies to better perform his or her job (not a technophobe)
- Thinks of ways to build better mousetraps
- Uses his or her experience to teach, coach, and mentor others
- Uses knowledge gained from other jobs to accomplish goals
- Likes to learn from younger colleagues as well as from older, more experienced colleagues
- Shares wisdom
- Motivates others
- Mentors colleagues
- Welcomes feedback and accepts better, faster, cheaper, more innovative and flexible ways of getting the job done
- Asks for help as needed
- Still takes leaps of faith
- Learns from encountering mistakes and speed bumps
- Embraces cultural differences

- Agrees to disagree agreeably
- Respects new ideas, investigates reasons behind decisions and suggestions
- Steps outside his or her comfort zone, "blows up the box" instead of just thinking outside of it
- Genuinely excited about being a member of an organization with so many age groups and cultures
- Can strategize how his or her job ties into organization goals and updates his or her experience to meet needs of a breakneck-speed workplace; ramping up ideas is not a problem—kicks things up a notch when required
- Realizes the workplace is not your grandfather's or great-grandfather's Oldsmobile anymore
- Reads to stay current and informed
- Never says, "I've been doing this job longer than you've been on the planet" or "I don't need a kid telling me what to do."
- Takes his or her legacy into serious consideration before taking action
- Does not count the days to retirement
- Wants to reinvent himself or herself
- Looks at every day as a way to reinvent himself or herself
- Goes back to school with gusto—studies Chinese or Russian, takes ballroom dancing lessons, becomes a professional chef just for the heck of it, and looks forward to bringing a fabulous dish to the next department potluck
- Sees the younger generation as the hope for tomorrow

- Asks younger employees for their input and suggestions on how to make the workplace more efficient and enjoyable
- Sees age as simply how many times the earth has revolved around the sun—exhibits a "we're all in this together" attitude
- Offers to break bread with people from other cultures and nationalities, invites people to lunch
- Asks others to share their perspectives, appreciates an entirely different viewpoint, agrees that disagreeing agreeably can be healthy for ongoing dialogue
- Is sensitive to those with disabilities or special struggles, personally and professionally, doesn't see these real-world issues as excuses but offers assistance and help
- Has learned from success as much as failure
- Encourages a global perspective
- Teaches others by example the virtues of common sense and good judgment
- Understands that boomers, seniors, and retired people often used to *live to work* but that now younger generations *work to live*; a redo sounds good!
- Sees the good in everyone and mines for the gold within each employee
- Instills pride in others
- Stands for something
- Exhibits work ethic and confidence younger workers want to learn from, without being preachy

Perfect Phrases for Gen Xers and Gen Yers (20- and 30-Somethings)

- Talks to supervisors, managers, and coworkers confidently about strengths but without sounding like he or she is bragging

- Talks openly about challenges and weaknesses without being overly needy or whining

- Understands that some people think this generation may have entitlement issues, but strives to demonstrate how he or she has earned a place through education, talent, and hard work, and plans to keep proving himself or herself

- Is assertive and pushes the envelope, takes risks, and seeks guidance when required

- Wants job to tie into interests wherever and whenever possible

- Is able to determine his or her strengths and helps others do the same

- Understands the concept of neutralizing weaknesses and that all jobs have difficult areas that have to be understood, but not necessarily mastered

- Has a well-thought-out answer to the question, "What are your plans for one year from now?"

- Answers this question confidently: "What do you love doing without tiring of it?"

- Has already begun to write a self-development plan on his or her own

- Appreciates others' differences and explores what piques their interest

- Recognizes other employees' interests outside the workplace and ties those interests into building a stronger team that meets their professional goals

- Seeks a wide variety of opportunities to familiarize himself or herself with the organization and with other colleagues

- Seeks out a workplace buddy or mentor, even if there's no formal mentoring program in place

- Pursues continuing education via on-the-job training, external organizations in his or her field, distance learning, e-learning, webinars, and teleseminars

- Networks with others in the same organization and globally on the Internet where there is opportunity to do so

- Networks with others in the same organization and outside the organization who do something different

- Benchmarks best practices of world-class organizations and applies and adapts those practices to improve processes on the job

- Is comfortable learning new things and challenging his or her existing talents—always wants to crank things up a notch

- Continues education through domestic and international studies—admires a global perspective and appreciates how small the world really is

- Is willing to take on new tasks and responsibilities with a positive attitude

- Craves new technology, has a "can't live without it" attitude

- Dreams big
- Anticipates and welcomes change
- Welcomes experienced workers' ideas and opinions, encourages improving processes
- Rather than bucking authority, finds ways to work together
- Knows that minding gaps and discrepancies brings people of all ages and stages of life closer together
- Understands how use of technology can help throughout his or her career
- Self-directed; takes action, then takes a break to recharge
- Uses intuition
- Takes time to be still, quiet, and think without interruption
- Blends e-mailing, IMing, texting, tweeting, and Facebooking into the workplace
- Welcomes new learning opportunities
- Enjoys learning from others
- Is excited to be on board
- Understands what the organization's purpose is and his or her part in making it happen
- Uses the organization's equipment responsibly, takes a hands-on approach when required
- Has a good work ethic, understands the importance of core values
- Is punctual and respectful of people's time
- Has an extremely positive attitude and influences others to have a positive attitude

- Wears appropriate clothing for the task at hand
- Uses appropriate language
- Takes responsibility for work; owns up to mistakes
- Is honest and sincere
- Contributes to the success of the organization
- Accepts feedback responsibly and appropriately
- Communicates effectively with both peers and managers
- Is mature
- Uses age-appropriate language; may be more casual in sentence structure and overall demeanor, but is sharp, articulate, and exudes a contagious attitude
- Does not behave like a victim or a martyr, nor does he or she encourage that behavior in others
- Has good personal hygiene, cares about his or her appearance; is well groomed and dresses appropriately for the job
- Enjoys meeting others with similar career interests
- Recognizes that bad behavior should not be rewarded
- Uses the "instant gratification" of short-term goals to help manage the journey toward long-term goals
- Using strengths of knowing technologies to grow skill sets
- Sees himself or herself as always being upgradable, looking to improve, grow, and nurture his or her abilities
- Welcomes learning opportunities from other cultures and levels within the organization, seeks to find out what makes people tick

- If he or she doesn't have a passport, shows interest in getting one
- Uses good judgment and common sense
- Likes feeling empowered, then does something with it
- Understands and knows the organization's mission and vision, then adds a new twist or spin on the message that freshens it up
- Uses his or her need for speed and instant gratification to get things done on the job
- Stands for something
- Not interested in drama or distracted by "needy" people
- Wants to give back and make a difference

Perfect Phrases for Organic Employee Development: The Natural Evolution of a Career

- Appreciates intrinsic motivation, leadership, teamwork, self-development, coaching, and more—it's got to come from within first and then grow
- Is a boundaryless thinker
- Does what comes naturally and applies it to the latest trends
- Clearly sees that with organic development of talents and resources, old ways become extinct—the way drugstore film development evolved to higher levels of technology and photo transmission now occurs at lightning speed
- Embraces speedy decision-making opportunities
- Negotiates from instinct and evolving knowledge
- Embraces spontaneity to advance on the job and in his or her field
- Eager to jump on with new, and sometimes even controversial, learning opportunities
- Learns well from others, studies neurolinguistic programming as a communication tool, examines people's behaviors and wants to know more about them
- Appreciates the value of authenticity
- Appreciates honest and genuine feedback, knows phony flattery when it's happening and is not pleased by it
- Initiates change and does not equate it with loss
- Listens well

- Accepts advice from seasoned colleagues
- Learns new technologies from younger colleagues, then writes a thank-you note—demonstrating appreciation is organic and natural
- Communicates from the heart
- Is comfortable in his or her own skin
- Has a good work ethic that's evolved from family traditions, immigrant roots, and just hardwired in DNA
- Is always evolving
- Career is an organic outgrowth of all he or she has learned and accomplished and all that he or she will become
- Envisions the future and all the possibilities, then is able to describe it vividly, painting a picture that others can get excited about and see themselves as part of
- Senses things intuitively and pays attention
- Has made it where he or she is because of decisions he or she has made; is accountable
- Follows his or her "true north" and isn't disappointed with the results
- Instinctively follows innovative career-pathing options and chooses the high road at all times
- Tries to blend life's many demands, not balance them like dinner plates spinning on a long stick in the air—we all have different capacities as to what we can handle responsibly without "dropping the plate."
- Enjoys finding organic and natural ways to find equilibrium at work and at home

- Wants to ignite intrinsic passion and activate natural talents and greater potential
- Thinks "able" even if he or she appears "disabled" to others

Multicultural and Diverse Workers

- Recognizes the importance of diversity and appreciating and learning from others' differences in a global workplace
- Realizes how very small this planet is and the need to be careful of who he or she might impress or offend along the way
- Accepts and relishes cultural differences
- Networks with others from different countries, often in same field, but seeks networks outside of his or her field too
- Overcomes biases, prejudices, and language barriers, regardless of upbringing
- Welcomes learning about other cultures—reads one international publication a month, watches BBC, or listens to international radio broadcasts
- Likes to travel, has a passport (in the United States, less than 4 percent of the population have one)
- Shows interest in things outside his or her own backyard
- Speaks more than one language, or self-studies a foreign language with a CD or online program
- Breaks bread (eats meals) with people from other cultures as a way to find commonality

- Seeks commonality to close gaps of understanding and tolerance
- Appreciates individuality
- Learns from others by asking questions about their culture such as, "What is Ramadan about?" or "When is Diwali, and what do you do during this time?"
- Participates in multicultural events in the workplace to lend support and increase understanding
- Reads about other cultures to gain an understanding of the depth and breadth of humanity
- Has friends from other countries
- Is interested in geography, takes time to study maps and globes
- Has lived in other countries, has thought to one day live in another country
- Gets along with colleagues
- Is articulate and confident, tries to speak and understand other languages, helps others with their English
- Works locally, acts globally
- Builds relationship bridges and helps people get over them

Beginner, Entry-Level, and Returning-to-Workplace Workers

- Learns how others in the same field do what he or she does, takes away good ideas, and learns to adapt and apply them quickly

- Asks to tag along to meetings to observe, listen, and learn
- Goes the extra mile to earn respect and build a reputation for reliability
- Learns fast and teaches others what she or he knows
- Appreciates and responds to being recognized for a job well done
- Interested in dress-for-success ideas, asks for feedback on appropriate dress and appearance
- Takes time to investigate the culture of the organization before starting a job
- Actively listens to others
- Seeks job satisfaction as well as pay
- Desires to follow his or her passion and build on his or her core competencies and strengths
- Shows eagerness to neutralize his or her weaknesses without detracting from his or her inner calling and natural strength-based skills
- Is open to learning and implementing new skills, tools, and techniques he or she may not have been exposed to
- Doesn't assume anything is too difficult
- Understands that the "real" learning begins when a training class has ended—when information can be applied on the job
- Applies new ideas readily
- Asks others to share their stories and ideas
- Contributes to a "safe" and confidential learning and working environment, does not gossip or create drama

- Understands the value of earning others' trust
- Takes advantage of all continuous learning opportunities
- Shares the credit for successful outcomes with others
- Wants to learn to be a stronger interviewer for future opportunities
- Finds transferable skills from home or hobbies that will apply to the workplace
- Not afraid to use life experiences to excel in the workplace
- Asks continually, "What can I do to improve on this next time?"
- Manages relationships between personal and professional life
- Seeks opportunities to familiarize himself or herself with the organization, takes initiative to do so; asks to see the annual report and asks someone to explain parts not easily understood
- Seeks out a workplace buddy or mentor, or calls a friend in the same field for advice and guidance every few months
- Pursues continuing education via cutting-edge job training, external organizations in his or her field, distance-learning programs, and investigating best practices within the industry on a regular basis, keeping current on the competition
- Uses benchmarking practices regularly
- Is organized, gives attention to detail without getting bogged down

- Stays out of the "drama zone" and other people's business
- Networks with personal contacts, business contacts, friends of friends who have contacts; makes cold calls and e-mails people he or she has never met to get information and insights; requests informational interviews with influential people in his or her field of work
- Is comfortable learning new things, looks for ways to step outside his or her comfort zone and take risks with new approaches
- Is creative in branding his or her name and expertise
- Has established himself or herself as a subject-matter expert in his or her chosen field to some degree, even if it's been in a volunteer capacity or as a hobby
- Is willing to take on new tasks and responsibilities outside his or her comfort zone
- Embraces new technology and offers to take classes and self-directed learning steps to learn and grow
- Understands the enormous value of better understanding and grasping technology and how that understanding can specifically help him or her throughout an entire career to move onward and upward
- Is excited to have learning opportunities and enjoys continuous learning
- Is genuinely enthusiastic and excited to be on board and part of the team

- Understands what the employer's purpose is and the importance of his or her part in making it happen
- Has goals and a plan to achieve those goals
- Has a strong work ethic and core values
- Is punctual and considerate of other people's time
- Comes to work on time and is rarely absent
- Has a supergreat attitude and spreads positivity
- Honors himself or herself, exhibits healthy self-esteem, but is not overly confident or cocky
- Is humble
- Gives others honest and sincere feedback and compliments
- Takes responsibility for work and outcomes
- Owns up to mistakes, shares his or her mistakes with others to prevent them from making the same mistakes
- Practices authentic behavior, is honest and sincere
- Contributes to the success of the organization on many levels
- Accepts and appreciates feedback; uses feedback responsibly and appropriately
- Communicates effectively with both peers and managers
- Makes eye contact with everyone, smiles
- Is mature
- Is professional
- Uses good judgment and common sense on a daily basis
- Embraces, enjoys, and participates in multicultural workforce teams and celebrations

- Knows presentation skills will be essential in the future, joins an organization such as Toastmasters

Mid-Level Leads, Supervisors, and Managers

- Shows mental readiness and the right attitude for making the transition from a beginner position to a mid-level lead, supervisor, or manager position
- Wants to hire for attitude and train for skill
- Builds relationships and builds bridges where there are gaps
- Seeks to take on greater responsibility overall
- Strives for diplomacy
- Is aware of the professional image he or she exudes
- Uses tact
- Prepares answers in advance
- Wants his or her success to contribute to the team's success
- Has solid writing skills and articulate verbal skills
- Learns to manage what he or she does with time available, not so much focused on hours in a day
- Encourages best practices performance
- Seeks individual equilibrium and balance between home life and work life
- Continuously learns how to manage varying relationships with others
- Gives respectful, appropriate, and positive feedback
- Receives and accepts feedback nondefensively

- Asks for constructive input and criticism, realizes feedback is the only way to grow and develop talent
- Steps outside his or her comfort zone to learn new skills helpful to managers (for example, learning to use new software to create a department budget)
- Walks the talk of "open-door policy"
- Sees value in workplace diversity
- Takes time to understand HR legalities and processes
- Delegates when necessary
- Finds rewards in work
- Clearly directs and instructs others
- Has faith in the staff to do their jobs to the best of their ability
- Welcomes teaching opportunities
- Challenges workers
- Learns new ways to mentor and coach
- Embraces learning how to manage others
- Attends networking functions
- Seeks learning opportunities in a variety of sources such as teleseminars, online classes, in-person classes, and seminars
- Thinks strategically
- Leads meetings without wasting others' time
- Motivates with praise in progress
- Inspires others, gets buy-in, builds loyalty

Upper-Level and Senior Managers

- Lists human capital as the most important asset on the organization's balance sheet
- Is an expert at developing top talent
- Encourages humor and fun in the workplace
- Leads others to grade their own performance
- Practices meaningful delegation
- Understands fundamental marketing
- Strives for outstanding customer care and excellence
- Uses diplomacy and discretion
- Knows when to keep things behind closed doors
- Is able to restore order and avoid chaos when unexpected or emergency situations arise
- Always tries to improve workplace processes with ongoing input from all workers, at all levels
- Is familiar with finance and accounting procedures, understands company's annual report, and shares accurate information with employees
- Hones critical thinking skills
- Presents range of various outcomes
- Is creative and innovative in his or her approach to leadership
- Understands return on investment (ROI)
- Encourages training and can measure results for senior leadership
- Always evaluates situations before taking action

- Seeks to understand and sharpen project management skills
- "Walks the talk," realizes hypocrisy is unacceptable
- Manages relationships first, not just tasks
- Inspires shared vision and goals of the organization
- Capitalizes on raw talent
- Blends home life and work life well
- Empowers colleagues, does not micromanage
- Welcomes and invites feedback from others
- Embraces learning opportunities, regardless of source
- Gives credit where credit is due
- Rewards good work
- Focuses on employees' skills and strengths
- Nurtures employee growth
- Encourages colleagues to take risks
- Welcomes opportunities to develop employees' skill sets
- Encourages employees to seek new and innovative ways to learn and grow
- Nurtures relationships among colleagues and team
- Respects all administrative support
- Knows how to put people's strengths to work
- Turns good performers into top talent
- Gives workers the benefit of the doubt
- Believes in second chances
- Understands human behavior

Director, Executive, and VP-Level Leadership

- Understands and accepts legal accountability of position
- Respects his or her position and tremendous influence as a leader
- Respects and honors others
- Practices servant or bottom-up leadership—an inverted pyramid of the traditional hierarchy
- Adopts a leadership style that generates heightened performance, intelligent decision making, and improved productivity among workforce
- Has deep self-awareness
- Demonstrates humility, enforces ability
- Faces down fears, instills courage in others
- Exemplifies passion for the work and exhibits a high energy level
- Inspires collaboration and shares credit with others
- Diagnoses problem issues promptly before they become big problems and takes steps to solve the situation without delay
- Makes hard, fast, smart decisions
- Keeps things affordable and actionable at all times
- Always looks for leadership of the future
- Has his or her job replacement in mind and builds strong talent pools in all departments
- Retains good talent because he or she nurtures and grows people first and foremost
- Finds out what motivates the troops and fuels that motivation daily

- Empowers others to higher levels of performance and productivity
- Is well equipped to optimize organizational performance in both good and bad economic climates
- Has weathered and survived many organizational changes
- Works well with executive level teams
- Is an inspiration and sets an example for all employees
- Employees are proud to call him or her their leader
- Knows how to use power and influence to achieve goals and help others
- Has built or been part of extraordinary teams
- Differentiates between various management talent levels and top leadership talent
- Knows what's required for success in the 21st century
- Has a solid succession plan in place
- Has a selected short list for his or her replacement, even if retirement is years away
- Is not fazed by change
- Has consistent leadership style
- Shows conviction of beliefs
- Prepares people and the organization for change
- Knows the importance of emotional intelligence (EQ) to top talent development and leadership
- Demonstrates passionate purpose
- Facilitates the strengths of others to grow top talent and neutralizes weaknesses

- Enjoys leading
- Sustains his or her individual success
- Implements performance intelligence
- Is a tough negotiator with successful track record
- Discovers what the organization should not be doing and stops doing it
- Values human capital as the organization's greatest asset
- Tells the world who he or she is by how he or she communicates
- Is considered a voice of leadership for the industry
- Has experienced failure and learned from it
- Explores the market and keeps a growing market share
- Drives new products, research, and development; keeps the pipeline of innovation full and moving forward
- Builds organizational profits and loyalty through internal and external customer relationships
- Knows strong presentation skills are priceless
- Encourages everyone to make presentations and join Toastmasters or similar organizations
- Recognizes there's a balance between home life and work life
- Develops staff by giving opportunities for growth
- Knows and calls employees by name
- Learns from more technologically savvy colleagues
- Embraces new ways of doing things
- Uses strengths and experience to help others advance their skills

- Motivates others
- Teaches, guides, and mentors colleagues
- Nurtures and develops relationships
- Appreciates that everyone has something to contribute
- Has clarity about purpose
- Knows what each employee brings to the table
- Encourages the best in people
- Lives by the Golden Rule: treat others as you would be treated
- Accepts and embraces cultural diversity
- Creates long-term strategies
- Knows short-term goals and encourages team to meet them
- Encourages team members to work the plan
- Embraces two-way communication
- Accepts feedback, even when at the top
- Knows when to "stop the car and ask for directions"
- Takes risks and encourages colleagues to do the same
- Takes chances on people
- Promotes a friendly work environment
- Requires an honest workplace
- Trusts employees
- Empowers employees to make decisions and to do their jobs
- Does not micromanage
- Knows how to communicate good and bad news appropriately

- Knows when to cut losses when a plan isn't working
- Encourages colleagues to seek their own solutions
- Knows one person doesn't have all the answers
- Encourages colleagues to achieve goals but doesn't scold if they fall short
- Provides opportunities for training and professional development to all employees
- Takes responsibility for decisions made
- Coaches effectively
- Ensures safe and communicative work environment
- Values stakeholders as much as shareholders
- Has mentors
- Has great sense of humor
- Works closely with IT department
- Makes technology user-friendly when possible so that everyone can be included in new learning opportunities

Perfect Phrases for Managers Who Want to Bring Others Up to Speed

- We need to talk . . .

- What do you think about . . . ?

- How would you like to try . . . ?

- May I tell you something?

- I'm going to give you something to check out and then get back to me on.

- I'd like to share something with you . . .

- You may or may not be aware of the situation at hand, but . . .

- I noticed something you should know about . . .

- Let's discuss this when you have a moment.

- I sent you an e-mail / text / voice mail about . . .

- Here's who you should talk to as soon as possible in order to catch up . . .

- Here are some resources that will help you enormously and help you to move things forward faster.

- Check this website out and read this; let's talk strategy tomorrow.

- You're moving in the right direction, but here's how you can accelerate the process . . .

- I need you to kick things up a notch; let's discuss the specifics and get you on a time tracker.

- Time is critical. How quickly are you willing to move on this?

Elevate Someone Within the Department

- You're ready to move up. How can I help you?

- It's time to take a leap of faith and step outside your comfort zone.

- What you need is a revised career plan; here's what we can do for you.

- You've mastered your current position; let's take things to the next level.

- You're ready for new responsibility . . .

- The leap is all that matters; the rest is incremental.

- Don't be afraid to overcommunicate; this will extinguish rumors.

Describe Someone Ripe for Elevating

- Embraces new challenges with gusto

- Learns quickly and retains information, does not repeat the same mistake twice

- Wants to move up in the organization; eager to get out there and do something big

- Doesn't fear success

- Cares about others first and fuels others' motivation to improve

- Appreciates mentors and coaches, thanks them and asks for harder lessons to learn

- Asks for coaching and advice continually

- Seeks out upward opportunities; knows that opportunities missed are options picked up by others

- Interviews for a more advanced job to get experience

- Uses interviews to learn and to show his or her desire to advance
- Sees everything as an opportunity for growth
- Sees *risk* as a four-letter word for success
- Is not afraid of success
- Sees difficulties as life's classroom for learning and advancement
- Demonstrates pride in both small and large projects
- Makes people feel included and part of something bigger than themselves
- Says yes to opportunities big and small
- Thrives on change and unforeseen challenges

Prepare an Employee for Advancement

- Reward hard work
- Be prepared for peers' responses to your advancement; here are tools to help you handle this
- Provide necessary resources to do the job successfully
- Give authority and allow employees to take the reins
- Relax, take it a step at a time
- If failure occurs, uses it as a learning opportunity, debrief
- Encourage higher learning and advanced degrees
- Give praise in progress, not just once a year or at the end of a major project
- Build in small wins along the way
- Focus on employees' talents and natural gifts, not their weaknesses and failures

- Give everyone a second and third chance for success—think Walt Disney!
- Take time to excavate talent, nurture it, and grow it
- Notice when an employee is striving for advancement or promotion
- Instill hope
- Take baby steps when required; take giant leaps when appropriate
- Recognize when an employee is ready to move on and move up
- Provide incentives where appropriate; little things like a half-day off, pizza party, acknowledgment before the team, or a thank-you note go a long way
- Never ask someone to do something you wouldn't do yourself
- Know mentoring and training isn't telling and commanding
- Invite the person to meetings with upper-level management
- Encourage reading
- Encourage going to seminars
- I've noticed you've been working hard lately, and I'd like to move you into a position with more responsibility where you can use your newly developed / polished / increased skills.
- You've mastered your position / skills in your job . . .
- Would you like to teach your associates what you learned at the teleseminar you attended?

- How do you upgrade yourself on an annual basis?
- How will you be better this year than last year?
- What resources do you need to perform at an even higher level?
- How do you define your performance intelligence?
- What is your capacity? How much can you handle?
- Whom do you depend on in a crunch? Can this person help you now to advance to the next level?
- What motivates you to your highest level of productivity?
- How important is compensation? Do perks make a difference? What do you place great value in as an employee?
- Do you feel recognized for your efforts?
- Keep the big ideas coming.
- What team members should be part of your next big project?
- How do you work with . . . ?
- How important is formal coaching to you? Who would you like to coach or mentor?

Groom an Employee for a Replacement Position

- Notices when employee masters skills, details what they are doing
- Recognizes when an employee is ready to move on and move up, takes action at the right time
- Encourages employee to attend professional development events

- Attends networking events with the employee
- Sets an example
- Seeks out new learning opportunities for others
- Learns from others and asks for their input
- Employee consistently meets deadlines
- Exceeds expectations
- Is friendly and easy to work with, a team player
- Demonstrates flexibility and can multitask and blend several projects at a time
- Needs someone to believe in him or her and say so
- Sets people up for success
- Does not use performance evaluation as a tool of destruction
- Chooses to use performance building for employee development
- Lets the employee help to create an employee development plan that works for him or her
- Follows up on milestones reached
- Documents and tracks successes and builds on strengths every day

Help an Employee Re-Create a Failed Development Plan

- Handles rejection respectfully and appropriately
- Decides to learn from rejection
- Does not pout / handles with maturity
- Willing to take baby steps to get to the big win next time

- Mantra: no whiners, no martyrs
- Is positive and constructive in sharing and accepting criticism and feedback
- Welcomes the opportunity to help
- Asks for help, admits needing help
- Accepts help
- Avoids self-destructive behavior
- Quickly learns failure is the only classroom that exists
- Does not allow himself or herself to be manipulated
- Shares information willingly
- Recognizes when a task isn't going according to plan
- Redirects efforts voluntarily
- Is not afraid to try a different direction
- Gives others a chance to find their own answers
- Gives others a chance to discover solutions on their own
- Celebrates mistakes to ensure a more positive future outcome for all

Help Teams Create a Plan and Then Work the Plan

- Suggests employee provides a template for an employee development plan, then reviews the plan with the employee and helps to enhance it
- Welcomes new ideas
- Brainstorms effectively, brain drizzling is not allowed
- Has employee define his or her meaning of "performance"
- Understands tasks at hand

- Offer your definition of performance and recognize any discrepancies
- Demonstrates confidence
- Is a self-starter, takes initiative
- Team members contribute equally
- Initiates team discussions
- Encourages team to recognize roadblocks and identify solutions together
- Facilitates successful employee development
- Welcomes new ways of decision making and creative thinking
- Uses good judgment and lots of common sense
- Communicates with respect to employees at all levels
- Communicates in a timely manner, doesn't wait for things to fester
- Gives feedback to the team
- Accepts feedback from the team
- Speaks clearly and without excessive emotion to convey his or her point
- Treats all team members with respect
- Recognizes everyone has something to offer
- Acknowledges problems and delays and acts upon them before productivity is affected
- Stays on task
- Stays on schedule
- Listens to and acts upon suggestions

- Recognizes that there may be more than one solution to a task
- Knows when to limit discussions so solutions can be acted upon
- Encourages the team to take good ideas and run with them

Help Build Confidence Levels Among Employees

- Welcomes the opportunity to encourage others
- Delegates appropriately
- Does not micromanage
- Encourages independent thought and action
- Sees coaching as part of his or her job
- Involves employees at every level
- Inspires others
- Encourages employees to take risks
- Rewards employees for taking risks / improving skills / excelling at tasks
- Gives positive feedback
- Bestows kudos
- Sees potential in others
- Is patient
- Explains details
- Teaches others
- Recognizes that making mistakes is part of risk taking
- Is open to building a better mousetrap
- Encourages free thought

- Welcomes opportunities to help others find their own solutions
- Welcomes new ideas

Conduct Employee Development Planning from a Distance (Virtual Managers)

- Is not intimidated by virtual team development or employee development from a distance
- Understands how work is now distributed across geography and across industries
- Builds stronger relationships within organizations to keep distance workers in the loop
- Knows importance of stronger vendor relationships, from Budapest to Bozeman
- Puts new emphasis on knowledge management and its applications
- Inspires collaborative work habits from a distance
- Harvests the ideas of people spread out geographically so that everyone in the organization, regardless of location, can learn and prosper
- Shares experiences from all cultures
- Uses netiquette (online etiquette) to maintain common courtesies and manners from a distance
- Manages and influences a whole spectrum of workers in multiple modes
- Integrates exciting new virtual practices, new systems, groupware, Internet, intranet, and whatever else is coming on the scene

- Sees himself or herself as a futurist
- Knows virtual teams will form and re-form continuously and encourages that change
- Won't let people get "stuck" in the mind-set of distance being an obstacle
- Promotes a paradigm shift to thinking of distance employee development as just better use of technology dovetailed with better understanding of human nature, even if it's not face-to-face
- Manages time well, knows how to prioritize
- Can work seamlessly with teams in various time zones, domestically and internationally
- Stays on task from a distance
- Virtually attends meetings and calls on a timely basis
- Lets others know if a project falls behind
- Knows bad news doesn't improve with age
- Has a good attitude about virtual employee development
- Works well alone and still enjoys collaboration
- Knows when to seek and use help from a distance
- Manages distractions
- Takes time to understand the culture of each virtual location where employee development is taking place
- Is positive about everyone's personal and professional accomplishments
- Uses time wisely to develop talent at every level
- Emphasizes the importance of meeting deadlines, time zone to time zone

- Identifies opportunities of a virtual team and shares them with everyone
- Focuses on the positive of employee development opportunities worldwide, not just on-site
- Plans get-togethers when appropriate at different locations around the country or world
- Knows how to turbocharge a virtual working environment with technology and good communication skills
- Aligns resources to build strong virtual teams and talent on those teams
- Adjusts accordingly when effectiveness wanes
- Uses "speedback" (fast feedback, one or two sentences at a time) to keep people in the loop
- Uses online tools effectively
- Gives virtual talent latitude to get used to virtual career counseling and development planning
- Creates remote team and talent enthusiasm and excitement
- Thinks geographically distributed teams and talent are the future success of the organization
- Demonstrates flexibility and spontaneity in the virtual environment
- Does not procrastinate; e-mails and calls workers when events occur, or alerts them when help is required anywhere, anytime
- Has a designated workspace at home (San Francisco, for example) for 2 A.M. conference calls with workers in other time zones (such as Mumbai or Sydney)

- Has technology backups ready to access in an instant
- Provides simulated virtual scenarios for online employee and team development
- Resolves conflict from a distance using virtual communication techniques
- Applies creative brainstorming and mind-mapping techniques from anywhere
- Understands and applies successful elements of coaching talent and career development in a virtual environment

Get Creative

With these phrases you can start building a wide variety of employee development plans. Select phrases for individual plans that best suit the growth needs of the people.

Get creative! Add phrases to different categories, rewrite a phrase, or expand an idea that best suits the personality of the group or the person you are coaching along. Select and utilize those that meet your organization's training needs, while complying with your organization's culture and individuality, then insert innovative ideas and approaches you glean from the phrases into a format that works best for you and your talent pool.

Use the phrases in this section to build onto, or simply enhance, an existing employee development program that needs sprucing up. Select phrases that turbocharge all of your employee development initiatives and dovetail them with employee suggestions and new approaches that put talent to work at its best.

Keep these phrases in mind as you read on to Part 2, which explores world-class employee development plans and the tools top talent uses to create them. Experiment to see where you can mix and match phrases for stronger, more powerful employee development plans.

Part 2

What the Best Do Better than Anyone Else

World-Class Managers Always Enrich Their Environment

If you've read this far, I'm confident that by now you have discovered some useful ideas, practical phrases, important lists, stories, and real-world examples that you can immediately take away and use on the job to create your own unique and exciting employee development plans.

In this section of the book, you will find world-class best practices and motivating perks and phrases used for growing employees to greater success. The following bite-size chunks of helpful how-tos come from talented leaders who have been successfully developing people for a good many years, using a wide variety of techniques and approaches to motivate and grow talent in the workplace. I've asked many leaders whom I know personally and have worked with to share their insights and behind-the-scenes secrets in this book.

Some are famous names, others are not so well known, but all are notably effective in their unique, one-of-a-kind takes on employee development and succession planning strategies. All practice, in their own special ways, the power of fueling people potential and employee development. Each creates real-world career possibilities, day after day.

From Pixar to Zappos—Winning Companies' Strategies for Growing Talent

Here you'll find a diverse group of leadership advice, from the creative computer animators at Pixar to the zany customer-coddling workers at Zappos. Maybe you will recognize some of these names or have read their books and admire their innate talent for bringing out the best in others. Regardless of your familiarity with these experts, all of them have proven performance records when it comes to creating dynamite opportunities for their people, turbocharging the workplace with fresh and innovative ideas, and leaving their indelible imprint on the hearts, minds, and souls of those who are fortunate enough to work with them.

Their voices are heard in this section. Share their stories and ideas with your teams and spread the word! And remember, it's not about trying to imitate any one culture or management style—far from it! Here you can do a fast benchmarking exercise, glean the things you like, pass over what you don't like, and adapt the best-of-the-best ideas to fit your own organization's culture and needs for ongoing employee development success.

So where do these methods and interviews—some of them one-of-a-kind—come from? They come from all sectors of the workplace—businesses, professions, global communities, associations, government initiatives, nonprofit organizations, the Internet, ethics think tanks and academia, health care, finance, entertainment, and the publishing and professional speaking world, to name a few.

There also are organizations and managers listed here that I have yet to work with or meet in person. Yet I've studied and researched them for years, teaching case studies on some of their powerful people development strategies in well-known universities and colleges. Many I developed long-lasting relationships with when I wrote another McGraw-Hill briefcase business book called *Building a High Morale Workplace.* If you are looking to build employee morale and motivate people to do their best work, in good times and hard, check it out and use it along with the tools in this *Perfect Phrases* book. I guarantee you it will give a boost to all of your employee development planning experiences.

Have you asked yourself lately, "What am I doing, for the sake of my people, to boost morale and enrich my organization's environment?" As managers, we all need to give a lot of thought to how we are enhancing and enriching the workplace. So how do you reshape or enhance the many benefits of working for your organization? The days when an employee benefits package was all about the dental plan are over. In small ways and bigger ways, managers are getting more creative in providing employees with perks uniquely their own—perks that contribute to an ever-changing and more exciting global workplace. Some cost zero dollars. Some cost much more. It's up to you how you structure it.

Let's start here with the power of "perfect phrases" perks you might want to try and the quirky e-tailer Zappos—kickin' it up a notch when it comes to nurturing employees.

Zappos

Quirky is good in this culture. The famous e-tailer believes in the "psychic gratification" employees get from helping others. Call-center customer service reps are given tons of freedom— they are allowed to chat as long as they like with customers, write thank-you notes, or even send flowers to a customer. Top priority? Make emotional connections! Zappos hires positive people and then places them where positive thinking is reinforced! CEO Tony Hsieh offers employees a list of his Ten Commandments, which include the following:

- Create fun and a little weirdness
- Pursue growth and learning

Pixar

The Academy Award–winning computer animation studio seeks superfun, tireless talent! Its priority? To combine technology with world-class creative talent. The creators of animated movies such as *Finding Nemo*, *Toy Story*, and *Cars* advertise on its website (using a creative spin on the *Cars* movie) that they are always looking to expand their pit crew of talented employees and that their "creative mechanics" come in all shapes and sizes.

NetApp

This data storage and management company may ask prospective talent to share specific examples of a time when their values were challenged. Purpose? To find out whether someone has the integrity required to work there. Here are a couple of NetApp's most sought-after employee qualities:

- Collaborative environment—loners need not apply
- Leave your ego at the door

Google

Yes, in tough times it has cut some frills, but not to worry—Googlers still get awesome perks, such as free massages, on-site car washes and oil changes, and gourmet meals.

Dell

"Employee commitment to revolutionary innovation." Dell offers resources employees will need to reach their loftiest career goals. Here are some of Dell's most sought-after employee qualities:

- Teammates inspiring greatness in each other
- Takes energy-smart, green initiatives
- Sees bright future for those with integrity, teamwork, and a passion for technology

The Ritz-Carlton Hotels (Marriott International)

This top company pledges an employee promise to:

- Apply the principles of trust, honesty, respect, integrity, and commitment
- Nurture and maximize talent to the benefit of each individual and the company
- Foster a work environment where diversity is valued, quality of life is enhanced, and individual aspirations are fulfilled
- Empower each and every worker with immediate authority to spend up to $2,000 on the spot, without additional management approval, to fix any guest's problem at the hotel.

AFLAC

AFLAC offers employees on-site day care, which includes two centers and more than 500 children, at a modest average cost of $352 a month to the employee.

Second shift workers use the benefit too. Day care hours extend to 11:30 P.M. Twelve weeks at full pay are given to care for a sick child, parent, or spouse.

The Container Store

As an alternative to worker layoffs during the lean times, The Container Store froze salaries for everyone. In another strategy for developing top talent, the company offers employees approximately 100 hours of training a year.

Bank of Montreal (BMO)

Talk about an atypical financial institution. This bank's culture is all about innovation and people. With tens of thousands of employees worldwide, Bank of Montreal is one of the largest banks in Canada and North America. Employees are encouraged to develop a sense of proprietorship in their work. Here are a couple of the bank's other selling points:

- Strongly involved with employees' continuing education
- Committed to training and lifelong learning
- Under its HR umbrella, the bank's Career Center offers employees access to the bank's Possibilities Center (the name alone sums up the organization's unique approach to growing and developing talent to its highest potential).

Here's how Bank of Montreal describes its values:

- We draw our strength from the diversity of our people and our businesses.
- We insist on respect for everyone and encourage all to have a voice.

- We share information, learn, and innovate to create consistently superior customer experiences.

Netflix

More than 8 million customers strong, this movie-rental business revolutionizer gives seven great reasons to work for Netflix:

- Netflix delights people
- Large impact
- Outstanding people
- Big pay
- Rules annoy us
- Clear values
- Amazing future

Levi Strauss and Company

Levi Strauss encourages employees to work on "way-cool" projects. Managers match their employees' interests to exciting and challenging new projects that ignite passion for the job. One leader refers to "the care and feeding of talent" (meaning employees are not attracted to a company by tangibles alone).

J.M. Smucker

This leading company enriches employees' environment with ongoing job rotations to keep employees motivated and interested with ongoing changes in scenery and job responsibilities.

Intuit

In this ultragreen company, bottled water is banned. Here are some initiatives Intuit has implemented to align employees' values with the company:

- Mass-transit subsidies for employees, up to $100 a month
- Sets goal to reduce carbon footprint by 15 percent in three years
- Replaced its pickup trucks with electric vehicles

Whole Foods Market

This company enjoys an enthusiastic young workforce (28 percent of employees are under age 25). Here are some of Whole Foods' employee development strategies:

- Mentors team members through education and on-the-job experience
- Encourages participation and involvement at all levels of the business
- Fosters self-responsibility and self-directed teamwork
- Rewards productivity and performance
- Offers opportunities that grow with the people
- Best employee ideas are exported to the company's stores around the country.

Scottrade

Stock market craziness led to this firm's biggest profits. Here are some of Scottrade's employee development strategies:

- Bonuses maintained even in turbulent times
- Never had a layoff

- Wants to attract employees that can contribute unique talents
- Internships all year long, not just during the summer
- 22 percent of branch managers started as interns
- Hires on average 50 percent of graduating interns each semester

The Walt Disney Company

All new-hire orientation at Disney begins with building pride and morale. New hires attend a "Disney Traditions Class" where they are taught Disney's history, philosophy, values, and high-quality guest services. "Cast members" train on the job and attend decentralized skill-building classes. Learning is done in engaging and powerful ways, where employees are encouraged to keep learning and develop themselves. Learning opportunities are designed to build on the competencies and capabilities of the people.

Disney programs include:

- New-hire orientation
- Disney Dimensions, an executive development program
- Disney Way, designed to showcase the various Disney businesses to managers and above
- Disney ethics, integrity, and diversity programs
- Professional development
- Management / leadership development
- Computer skills
- Exciting e-learning programs that allow employees and Cast Members around the world to access learning opportunities at their convenience

In addition, the Walt Disney Company provides educational reimbursement for full-time employees and Cast Members.

DreamWorks Animation SKG

Lots of freebies!

- Fun wrap parties (completion of movie celebrations)
- Free gourmet breakfasts and lunches
- Rural Glendale, California, campus is surrounded by storyboards and movie characters like Bob from *Monsters vs. Aliens*

Boston Consulting Group

This premiere global management consulting group, with more than 60 offices worldwide, has greatly increased the recruitment of minorities, approximately 25 percent of staff. Here are some of its employee development strategies:

- Believes no two career paths are the same
- Offers formal training to support employees
- Provides informal training to stretch employees
- Initiates work-life balance with predictable time off
- Takes "grow further" approach to employee development
- Believes that a person's potential is only limited by talents and ambitions
- Provides experience to excel in numerous fields
- Offers 100 percent fertility treatment coverage

Here Come the Subject-Matter Experts!

President Abraham Lincoln believed that each of us could learn a great deal more from people who have different perspectives and viewpoints from ours than from the people who consistently agree with us or share our philosophies. This attitude demonstrates the power of servant leadership and how much we can learn from others' differences. It embraces diversity. This section of the book is dedicated to underscoring the importance of that message. You'll also find a fast way to benchmark the best others have to offer, while staying true to your own philosophies, core values, and individual style of management.

Job satisfaction in the United States has dropped considerably. According to the Conference Board (ConferenceBoard .org), a nonprofit global organization based in New York City, only 45 percent of workers in America are reporting job satisfaction. This figure is down more than 60 percent from 1987, and it is the lowest in more than 20 years.

This information should capture the attention of every manager and be the impetus to further examine each organization's employee and talent development planning options and then try to shape those options by creating a more engaged and motivated workplace.

The remainder of Part 2 describes the methods and ideas of some of the more than 100 organizations and people I have spoken with, dined with, trained, and interviewed for their perfect phrases, ideas, and amazing talents. All of these extraordinary people have been generous and thoughtful with their time and often with my nonstop queries, e-mails, texts, letters, telephone calls, and requests for one-on-one meetings.

Each person was selected to be in this book based on his or her unwavering commitment to creating a more joyful, respectful, humane, esteeming, high-spirited place for employees to work and grow their talents.

Get Employees to Say YES to Personal and Professional Development

Lawrence Polsky and Antoine Gerschel are experts in helping employees say YES to change and YES to employee and talent development. Their change leadership tools have been heralded on five continents and are detailed in their latest McGraw-Hill book, *Perfect Phrases for Communicating Change*. To face the challenges of change, your employees need the right attitude. Use the ideas in this section to help them develop that attitude.

The question comes down to how you can best design your culture's employee development strategies and take them beyond just "survival mode." The workplace has changed dramatically over the past two decades and will continue to do so. And that's a positive change. Great things are on the horizon for senior leaders, managers, supervisors, leads, and frontline workers who are willing to move their people past the natural resistance to change and start facilitating talent development to its ultimate peak performance and productivity.

If you're ready to make the necessary changes in order to keep up, ask yourself the following questions:

- What are the top talent behaviors I'd like to see?
- How does peak performance and productivity look in our workplace?

- Am I ready to say yes to talent development?
- How will I brand talent for ongoing employee development and succession?

Get Employees to Say YES to Employee Development Plans

Polsky and Gerschel use the YES acronym to describe the process they use to help employees accept change and development:

Y = **Why change?** Your employees' reason to change must be beyond your business case. It must be selfish (serve their personal interest), be very personal, and be very compelling for them—for example, keeping their job, getting a raise, or being eligible for career advancement.

E = **Expect emotional reactions.** Negative emotional reactions to change are normal. Have employees reflect on the emotional reactions they are having to the change. What are they scared of losing? What obstacles are they expecting?

S = **Surround yourself with other fun-loving YES! people.** Change is draining. Negativity, hard work, and obstacles are persistent. Make sure employees identify support they need. What friends and colleagues can mentor, coach, and advise them? What can you as their leader do to support them? What can they do to support themselves and reduce the stress of change?

Ask, "What's in It for *Them*?"

These experts say it is easy for employees to say YES to development when the development is in their self-interest. Take the example of allowing an employee to get an MBA through tuition reimbursement. The MBA is in the self-interest of the employee. The employee is motivated to get it done because it will help the employee advance his or her career in whatever job or company he or she is in. It is a no-brainer. The leader never has to remind or encourage employees to participate. They just do it.

However, getting employees to say YES to developing new skills for their current jobs can be a huge challenge for leaders. Take a common example of employees needing to learn new skills so they can use the new software that is being rolled out. "What do you mean I have to do it differently? We have done it this way for 15 years!" the employees may think or say. They delay taking the online tutorial. They get sick when the class is scheduled. They are freaking out as the "go live" date draws closer. They don't see what is in it for them. It is the age-old problem of resistance to change.

Create a Dialogue That Leads to YES

Here are some questions to consider and ideas for more powerful manager/employee dialogue that will help employees move past their resistance and say YES to development. This facilitation process will help you to easily guide the way.

■ **Do employees understand the business case for their changed behavior?** We all live in a changing environment. Getting employees to accept change starts with understanding the business needs for change. What is your business situation, and how is it changing to require them to develop new skills?

- **Can you sell the development to them?** Once you understand the business case, you need to think about how you will sell the change. Without employee buy-in and support, you will fall short in your change effort.
  - *Create a vision of success.* Describe what the employee will be doing differently? Saying? Feeling? What results will he or she be able to achieve?
  - *Get key stakeholders on board.* Identify the people in your organization who can help your employee succeed in learning this new skill. Then, indicate what kind of support you need from them and how you will get it. For each person identified, specify whether he or she can help by advocating for the development, supporting the development, and/or providing input on the development.
  - *Make your pitch.* Selling development requires a short, compelling pitch. Using your ideas above, come up with key words and phrases to get your points across to your employees in 60 seconds or less. What are their likely objections? What will you say to address them?

- **Do you have the kind of employees who ask, "What can I learn next?"** Walking through these questions will get employees on board. They will become engaged in their learning and develop new skills because they want to, not because you are telling them they have to. As a result, you can spend your time leading and employees can focus on learning. However, don't be fooled into thinking that going through these questions and steps once is enough. As in any change, employees will need reminding of their motivation, coaching, and cajoling to keep focused. If you keep at it, employees will be asking you, "What can I learn next?"

Lawrence Polsky and Antoine Gerschel are managing partners of PeopleNRG and can be reached at info@peoplenrg .com; or visit their website at peoplenrg.com.

Attitude Is Everything in Employee Development

If there were an Attitude Hall of Fame, Sam Glenn would be inducted! He's one of my favorite motivational speakers. They call him The Authority on Attitude™, and for good reason. He's the founder of EverythingAttitude, Inc., and publishes an award-winning quarterly magazine called *Attitude Digest*, considered the premiere workplace publication for inspiring workers' and their teams' best attitudes.

Sam has changed the face of employee and talent development across America, delivering more than 100 presentations a year to organizations that believe attitude is a vital ingredient to helping employees develop their talent and achieve success. His presentations to audiences as large as 75,000 drive home his powerful message that everyone needs a *Kick in the Attitude* every now and then to recharge his or her career, team, and life.

This year, in response to audiences' demand for Sam's one-of-a-kind workplace training programs, which underscore the messages of his keynote presentations, *Kick in the Attitude* and

Who Put a Lizard in My Lasagna?, Sam launched Go Positive™ seminars and training programs. Managers and supervisors agree that Sam's training programs have given their employees the boost they need to make the most of who they are using all that they've got.

Incorporating Attitude into Employee Development Plans

You can be the most educated, talented, and experienced person, but if your attitude isn't right, then the results won't be right. Our education, experience, and talents function *through* our attitude to achieve results. If an organization values growth and wants the best results from its people, then there has to be an intense focus on helping people get better—no matter how good, gifted, and great they are.

The reason achieving a real *Kick in the Attitude* in the workplace is vital is because when the people in the organization get better, the organization gets better. And it has to start with attitude. It doesn't take much to implement, but the force behind a company's attitude can rally the troops, while a poor attitude can defeat the best and most well-developed employee development plans.

There are three huge stumbling blocks that complicate achieving the goal of a positive company attitude:

- Organizations look at the budget and bottom line and think, *We can't afford workplace development. Our people are smart enough. They will get the job done.*

■ Leaders think, *Employee motivation is overrated. People are hired to work and should do what they are paid to do. If they don't like it, they can go find work elsewhere.*

■ The corporate culture reflects the attitude, *Workplace motivation takes up too much time and doesn't work the same for everyone.*

These are excuses and frequent phrases you hear from organizations that didn't fare well in the economic downturn and are now really struggling. In essence, the underlying theme amongst these companies is that they are complicating simplicity. Incorporating a positive attitude in the workplace is not hard or expensive.

Tips for Developing Employees' Confidence, Teamwork, and Job Satisfaction

■ **Have a reward and recognition system in place.** They teach you this at puppy training class. Catch your puppy doing something good and praise him quickly, so he keeps doing it! Many professional organizations will reward their employees for performing their basic responsibilities in a manner that is consistent with in-house objectives and expectations. Some companies do not feel it is appropriate to reward an employee for simply performing the responsibilities that are expected. Regardless of what type of reward or recognition system you have in place, the most important thing you can do to ensure employee motivation is to always recognize the fact that they are working according to expectations and acknowledge them in a positive way for doing so. It can be a simple e-mail saying,

"Thank you, Betty, for getting that information so quickly today! I am very grateful. Hope your day is going great!"

■ **Eliminate de-motivators.** Find out what bothers your employees, and do your best to address the problems. Maybe your star salesperson is tired of having the copy machine located by his or her cubicle. Can you move it to the hallway without much ado?

■ **Offer an incentive luncheon.** Invite a special guest speaker for those who achieve a certain level of achievement or attitude. I call it "attitudes for lunch."

■ **Have a personal and professional development library.** This is a simple and affordable way to keep your employees on the cutting edge. People desire to improve, but you have to put some options in front of them. This is one way to do it. When employees are commuting to and from work, they could be listening to information that makes them better. Provide books, audios, or videos.

■ **Demonstrate a positive attitude in leadership.** It's hard to expect a positive attitude of your employees if you are walking around complaining. Even if times get tough, be action oriented and find solutions amidst trials. Demonstrate to your staff that the way out of problems is to persevere and put your best foot forward.

■ **Invest in motivational training, and follow up.** A motivational keynote speaker can do wonders to kick off a large project or recharge a listless staff. Take it a step further and hire a trainer to come in for a full day or more to implement skills for employee development and change. If the attitude environment changed in your office, and your employees were able to face their day with a "can-do" attitude, how much more would your company achieve? How would that affect the bottom line? The investment is worth it!

Sam Glenn's new book, *A Kick in the Attitude: An Energizing Approach to Recharge Your Home, Work and Life* (Jon Wiley & Sons), is a great read and an essential tool for managers. It's an employee development road map that's smart, funny, and packed with no-nonsense attitude principles that activate people's potential. You can get lots of free helpful information at www.EverythingAttitude.com, or e-mail Sam at contact@ everythingattitude.com.

What a Leader Must Do to Develop People and Grow Talent

Brian Lewis has been leading teams in both the public and private sectors for almost 30 years. His genuine leadership style and focus on high performance has resulted in national recognition and, more important, colleagues who have followed him from one employment opportunity to another.

Brian is the executive director of the California Association of School Board Officials (CASBO), based in Sacramento, California. He's also the publisher of CASBO's highly acclaimed magazine, *California School Business*, in which he writes an entertaining and substantive monthly column and editorial.

Here is a partial list of what Brian believes a leader must do to develop people and grow talent:

- Genuinely want to know what team members think
- Genuinely want them to participate . . . be inclusive
- Genuinely want them to add value
- Genuinely want them to be, and empower them to be, an integral part of the process that determines your long-term goals and short-term tasks
- Acknowledge your own mistakes; it doesn't undermine your credibility—it builds it
- Nothing new happens without risk

Finally, Brian advises you to support your team members as individual professionals. Want the best for them, whether with your company or not. He says he has seen leaders sabotage a member of their team so as to prevent him or her from moving on to a new opportunity either within the organization or in another organization. People will come and go, especially the good ones. If you genuinely want what's best for them, support them in all ways to achieve their goals. If the time comes when you and/or your company can't offer them what they need to move forward, congratulate them, and then assist them. What goes around really does come around.

Nothing Undermines Success Faster than the Lack of Trust

Brian tells the following story to illustrate the need to trust employees:

"Some years ago I worked for a good man who had no clue about management, much less leadership. He was big and brusque and intimidating. I had been hired to take an 11-person team and build it into an effective operation. I learned an important lesson from him, though it took some time for it to hit me. I learned that when he hired someone, he didn't trust the person. He anticipated less than successful performance. He expected problems. He didn't believe in his people, and he didn't trust his people.

"I learned as a result of this experience. That is to say, I became conscious of the fact that I, when I hire someone, automatically trust the person and place my full confidence in him or her. It's about genuinely encouraging and expecting success and collaboration, not anticipating a lack of trustworthiness and standing by and waiting for failure."

What's real is that the employee in this situation perceives intuitively that the boss doesn't trust or believe in him or her. Nothing gets in the way of employee development faster than that lack of trust and support from a leader.

Volunteerism Helps Develop Employees . . . and Helps Your Company, Too!

Laraine Kautz is an active and involved volunteer who changes the world for the better, quietly and profoundly. Her strong conviction of service and giving caught my attention and led me to request her contribution to this book. For Laraine, it seems, that volunteering is not a choice; it's a responsibility to the planet. Her genuine commitment to serving others and her servant-leadership style of supervision and management remind me of something Muhammad Ali once said: "Service to others is the rent you pay for your room here on earth."

There's a New Zealand Maori proverb that goes, "With my resources and your resources, everyone will benefit." Kautz's personal and professional philosophy on growing talent and developing employees stems from her fierce dedication to volunteerism and its powerful ripple effect in communities, big and small, across the globe. Here is what Laraine had to say about employee development planning and the importance of including volunteerism in the equation.

Volunteering Mixes Philanthropy, Marketing, and Skill Development

Volunteering is at the intersection of philanthropy, marketing, and skill development. Volunteer-driven organizations benefit from an array of skills ranging from event planning, fund-raising, carpentry, cooking, and teaching to photography, writing, graphic design, accounting, board services, and beyond. Companies benefit from investing in their community and the increased visibility in an ever increasingly competitive economy. Employees benefit from the opportunity to hone underdeveloped skills and explore areas of interest while fostering positive relationships.

As an employer, ask yourself this question: *What does my company do to create positive long-term changes in my community and in the world of business?* The answer may result in a list, long or short, of organizations that you donate time, talent, or treasure to. If your company is not actively participating in volunteer activities for someone or something, it is time for you to make a list. One place to begin is to look at your company's vision and mission and identify which not-for-profit organizations have a mission or vision that is an extension of yours or perhaps just supports a cause that is near and dear to your heart. What does this have to do with employee development, you ask?

Find Out What Your Employees Are Great at—It Might Surprise You

To begin making meaningful connections for your employees, ask them to identify the top three or four things that they are great at. The first two or three should be directly related to their current position, while the remaining one or two should pertain to any aspect of their life.

I know a financial manager that can cook five star meals, a chemical engineer that trains a competitive cheerleading squad, and an insurance agent that sails boats. I am fixated on finding out about an entire person. The knowledge brings interesting metaphors, analogies, and wisdom to the table, as well as the added benefit of breaking down stereotypes. Long gone are the days of leaving work at work and home at home, so capitalize on this. Take the time to find out what your employees are great at; it may surprise you.

Second, ask your employees to identify the top three or four things that they like to do. Again, have them identify at least one item that does not pertain to their current position. A nurse I know likes to respond to cardiac arrest calls on any floor in her hospital. Although she often is not the first responder, she likes to watch because she feels it keeps her comfortable with and knowledgeable about the procedure. A postal carrier I know enjoys taking adult education classes at the local high school just because the course sounds interesting. And then there's an administrative assistant who likes to bake delicious treats for company and occasionally sells them at holiday craft fairs because it's relaxing and a fun way to make extra money. We have a tendency to make time for the things we like to do on the job because they are exciting, interesting, or fun.

Third, ask your employees which two things, pertaining directly to their position, they would like to strengthen, while you add a third item that fits the company or department's strategic goals.

The fourth and final step is to combine all of this new information and connect your employee with an invaluable volunteer experience. The experience should present an opportunity for the individual to use his or her expertise, be related in some way to the things he or she likes to do, and offer situations that challenge the employee to grow.

Remember, volunteering has a ripple effect that touches all in its path with a promising return on investment. Volunteering is good for your company, and it is good for your employees. Open up opportunities to employees at all levels of your organization. Opportunities are plentiful—they can be time-consuming, time-bound, or something in between. There is a match for everyone.

Perfect Phrases to Describe
How Volunteering Develops Employees

- Networking on your company's behalf and for themselves
- Brainstorming with industry experts
- Connecting with customers
- Reaching new demographics
- Sharpening their skills in a new environment
- Discovering new skills and capabilities
- Developing new or enhanced insight for company programs or projects
- Finding inspiration in doing good for someone or something
- Finding out about available resources or funding sources

I got the distinct impression that for someone like Laraine, the honor of giving is honor enough. For more information on the Dutchess County Workforce Investment Board, visit their website at www.dcwib.org. Laraine Kautz can be reached at Lkautz@dcwib.org.

An HR Thought Leader Brands for Talent

After 30 years in corporate human resources (HR) and talent management, Libby Sartain is now an active business adviser, board member, and HR "thought leader." She is the former chief human resource officer (CHRO) of both Yahoo! Inc. and Southwest Airlines and serves on the board of directors of Peet's Coffee & Tea, Inc. As principal of Libby Sartain, LLC, she is an active adviser to several start-up businesses and a much-sought-after subject-matter expert on employer branding and talent management. In 2005, *Human Resources Executive* magazine named her one of the 25 most powerful women in HR. Following are her thoughts on branding for talent.

Making Your Talent as Famous as Your Brand

Business competes for talent today in a free global marketplace in which traditional definitions of job and employee are increasingly outmoded. As a direct result, HR leaders must also change traditional ways of working in order to maintain their central role in the organization of the future.

While many influences are bringing about this change, perhaps the most important is the way in which the worker now approaches and engages with work. Workers today use the sensibilities of consumers to search for overall *work experiences* that not only provide a sense of connection and fulfillment, but also a part of their personal brands.

Career Development Plays an Essential Role

Career development is an essential part of that work experience. Leaders are discovering the important link between talented employees and delivering a brand promise to consumers. So part of that career development is the process a leader uses to connect workers to their role in delivering the brand promise and creating an organizational brand for talent that will thrive in the new talent marketplace and with the new consumer of work.

Sartain is the coauthor of *HR from the Heart: Inspiring Stories and Strategies for Building the People Side of Great Business* (AMA COM). You can reach her at www.LibbySartain.com, or e-mail her at Libby@LibbySartain.com.

More on Branding for Talent

MedAmerica Billing Services, Inc. (MBSI) is a company that brands for talent. As Libby Sartain explained, *branding for talent is the sure sign of a company as famous for talent as it is for its products and services.* And that's exactly what MBSI president and COO James V. Proffitt III has managed to do in an industry profession that could easily get locked down in the daily details of precision auditing, compliant coding, hospitalists' practices, custom data analysis, and electronic submission of claims. Here Proffitt and other members of MBSI's employee development team share their insights.

Developing Career Plans for Employees

Jimmie Proffitt emphasizes that you have to be out in front, focus, mentor, and be genuine! This leads to relationships with high levels of trust. Once you're there, just allow your employees to do their own thing. Employees need the latitude to "make it happen," and with the right relationship, learning, growing, and excellence is going to be the result.

First, you have to have integrity, honesty, and trust in the eyes of the employee, according to Proffitt. To help someone, he or she first has to trust your motives and believe in your advice. At that point, it's easy to discuss what's important, develop career plans, give constructive and honest feedback, memorialize action plans, and track progress via review sessions. Then if you need to have the "tough love" discussion, it's more likely to be accepted.

"MBSI requires active, intelligent, motivated, and trustworthy employees to make things happen day in and day out. Therefore, it's not enough to develop employees on the basics; we need them to develop their emotional intelligence (EQ), expand their knowledge base, and live for their fellow employees' success," says Proffitt.

Developing a Solid and Reliable Succession Plan

Stephanie M. Montanez, director of human resources, is passionate about the new succession plan she is helping to create for the company. She says that MBSI must initially identify internal employees or external candidates that have the proper skill sets and competencies required to do the jobs available and who are willing to be trained in other areas. MBSI is committed to providing the necessary training, employee development, and mentoring required to assist the person in his or her success in future roles.

"People will be great at what they do if they have consistency, repetition, praise, and challenges to grow. Self-enjoyment and excitement help people to advance, as well," says Montanez.

Growing Employees Who Faced
Initial Rejection for a Job Promotion

When Linda Fleming, director of billing operations, interviewed for a call center manager position, four internal candidates applied. Unfortunately, they were not selected. Linda describes her follow-up with these employees: "I offered to meet with each of them if they wanted specific feedback on their interviews. Two of the candidates took me up on the offer. We discussed their strengths and ways they could develop further in their areas of weakness. I then arranged a 90-day follow-up meeting to see what they had accomplished in that time. One person totally blew me away with everything she had taken the initiative to do and improve upon. If she applies for a management position with me in the future, I will seriously consider her for the job."

A Code of Conduct

Here are a few statements that capture MBSI's Code of Conduct

■ Honesty: We are straightforward and truthful in our conduct and speech.

- Integrity: Our word is our bond—we mean what we say and say what we mean.
- Respect: We value each person as an individual.
- Trust: We earn the confidence of others through teamwork and open, honest communication.
- Responsibility: We can be depended on to fulfill our obligations and duties to our coworkers, clients, communities, and families.

For more information about MBSI, visit its website at www .MedAmericaBilling.com. For information on employee development planning training and other MBSI management training programs offered worldwide, e-mail Stephanie M. Montanez, director of human resources, at MontanezS@MedAmerica .com.

The Importance of Ethics in Developing and Growing Talent

Dr. Karen Eriksen is the president and CEO of Eriksen Institute. She is a professional speaker and trainer who promotes development of ethical decision making and inspires people toward optimal values and behavior, while transforming families and businesses alike. She has written about the rising popularity of ethics courses at top B-schools, or business schools, around the world in recent years. These classes often have long waiting lists. Businesses have finally come to understand that if they want to be successful and increase profits, a good deal of achieving that end result will depend on employing and developing ethical people. Following are her thoughts on the role of ethics in employee development.

Ethical values such as trust, trustworthiness, integrity, fairness, and respect are fundamental to who we are and how we treat other people. Not only do managers and leaders need to operate from a clear ethical base because it is the right thing to do, but because the trickle-down effect means that if they don't operate ethically, their employees won't either.

Growth in Character as Part of an Employee Development Plan

Managers and leaders not only need to model behavior that reflects ethical values; they need to speak about values, offer recognition and promotion on the basis of values, plan training and meetings in which employees learn to apply ethical values to everyday situations, act to end unethical behavior, and require employees to include growth in character as part of their development plans.

Once a company has gone through some processes to become clear on the ethical values that they are going to adopt, stand for, post, have discussions about, etc., then managers and leaders could require employees to indicate in development plans how they would apply these specific values to their work.

For instance, if competence, fairness, and integrity were included in the company's values or mission statement, the employee could be required to indicate how he or she would actualize these ethical values in the plan:

- Assess daily work tasks to determine where increased competence is needed

- Increase competence by participating in relevant training programs or continuing education
- Become more aware of how to treat reports fairly and with integrity, for instance, by assessing the degree to which others believe I am acting fairly and with integrity (anonymous survey of reports, colleagues, and manager)
- After listing daily work tasks, document ways to increase fairness and integrity, set specific goals and target dates for doing so, and revisit goals on target dates during supervision

Important Action Steps for Employee Development

Here are some steps an employee can take to study and practice ethical behavior and to implement that behavior in his or her individual personal and professional growth plan:

- Become aware of laws and regulations that are applicable to his or her work
- Commit to acting within these laws and regulations and to attending regular continuing education related to them
- Commit to encouraging colleagues and requiring reports to act within these laws and regulations, to challenging unethical or illegal behavior upon becoming aware of it, and to blowing the whistle on anyone who fails to operate within the law and regulations
- Participate in periodic discussions with colleagues and managers related to conscientiousness in abiding by the laws, particularly considering how to manage ethical dilemmas (such as when different laws conflict or ethics and law conflict)

- Know the aspirational ethical values of the company (or help the company to develop them)
- Participate in training and discussions on applying these ethical values to the particulars of the job
- Participate in regular ethical dilemma discussions in which employees struggle with how to apply aspirational ethical values to develop the best options in difficult cases
- Aim to actualize these values on a daily basis, setting specific goals and objectives publically and on a regular basis
- Anonymously survey reports, colleagues, and manager as to success in actualizing these ethical values

Dr. Eriksen is a professional speaker and trainer who promotes development of ethical decision making and inspires people toward optimal values and behavior, while transforming families and businesses alike. Her presentations on *Aspirational Ethics for Everyday Business Life* are worth checking out at her website, along with her many books, leadership guides, and training programs. Visit www.erikseninstitute.com, or e-mail her at Karen@erikseninstitute.com.

Individual Development Planning: The Government Way

Martha Lambie is the deputy regional commissioner for the Denver Region of the Social Security Administration. She oversees the Denver Region's 53 field offices in six states. Martha is passionate and driven when it comes to employee development and succession planning.

Here, Martha Lambie outlines the evolution of the Denver Region's remarkable four-part employee development planning strategy.

Part 1: Succession Management

Succession management was identified in 2006 as a critical area that the Region needed to intentionally concentrate its efforts on. Our experience was that while we were in a better position in terms of recruiting and hiring new employees, we still were not seeing a great deal of interest on behalf of all employees in applying for jobs outside their respective offices. Considering the vast geographic area of the Denver Region, the six states of Montana, North Dakota, South Dakota, Utah, Wyoming, and Colorado, we knew it was critical to begin to at least lay the groundwork to first identify those employees who could fill leadership roles in the future while at the same time encouraging more mobility within the region.

To accomplish this, an employee development conference was planned. This was the first such conference of its type in the nation. The design of the Professional Enrichment Acquiring Knowledge (PEAK) conference was to equip employees for advancement by having sessions on completing applications, preparing for job interviews, dressing for success, informational session on career paths, and taking charge of your own career, to name a few.

Each employee pays his or her own way to the conference, which is spread over a day and a half. Executives from both the region and headquarters conduct the workshops or speak at the plenary sessions. A networking social event, which is optional, is held on the night between the two sessions and gives the employees the opportunity to interact with the executives. Since 2006 the conference has become an integral part of our succession management plan, with attendance growing to more than 150 this past year. Employees come from all over the region, and for those living in our more rural locations who are unable to attend, the sessions have been broadcast over a video network. The benefits we've seen from these conferences have been the excitement of employees and the number of applicants we now have for job openings.

Part 2: Achievement Plan

Another strategy that has been used is a development program that provides lower graded employees an opportunity to take on assignments outside their normal job duties that help them develop skill sets that build their résumés for potential promotion. This Denver Achievement Plan (DAP) has now been in existence for three years and is offered by managers to employees in all 53 offices throughout the region. It is a voluntary program with employee self-nomination. The participants develop an individual development plan (IDP) and work with a mentor throughout the one-year program.

Part 3: A Successful Management Development Program

The region also has a Management Development Program (MDP) that provides participants a one-year temporary promotion with work assignments outside their home offices. Assignments can and often are paid assignments away from home working either in the regional office or even at SSA's headquarters in Baltimore. In addition to the MDP the region enrolls candidates in the one-year developmental programs offered by the Office of Personnel Management (Colorado Leadership Development Program and Utah Leadership Development Program).

Part 4: Mentoring and Coaching for Success

The last initiative, in which Anne Bruce has played an integral part, is the development of a mentoring program. In the past the region would ask for mentor volunteers and pair them up with candidates in one of the above programs. There was little or no guidance given to the mentors, not to mention expectations set for the involvement of a mentor in a candidate's development. We now offer vendor training to all mentors/mentees as part of the program orientation. We also have included mentor training in our management meetings as a workshop with training being provided by a cadre of instructors.

Following this interview with Martha Lambie, I spoke with Nancy Berryhill, the Denver Regional Commissioner. She wanted me to emphasize that along with the Social Security Administration, she is personally committed to providing employees with tools and resources to help them achieve their individual career aspirations. Berryhill predicts that in the next several years there will be numerous opportunities for career and employee development planning and advancement as agency leaders retire or advance in their own careers. She enthusiastically shares this credo with all employees: "We must depend on you, our best resource."

Next, read in Part 3 how you as manager can start turbocharging the workplace with perfect phrases that put employee development into motion!

Part 3

**Perfect Phrases
That Activate Employee
Development Plans**

All the perfect phrases in the world will not be enough for a manager or supervisor to structure an effective employee development planning system without a specific call to action or built-in activation mode. This part of the book is devoted to some of the perfect phrases that can easily become an employee's call to action.

There Is No *Abracadabra* in Employee Development Planning

Here's the upshot. There is no such thing as *abracadabra* when it comes to transforming your people into tomorrow's top talent. Despite the mythical pixie dust that only exists in fairy tales, there is no magic trick or special potion to sprinkle on employees in hopes of creating extraordinary talent who can handle all of the challenges they ultimately will face. Employee development planning is hard work.

Take the wellspring of phrases in this book—phrases that I hope have stimulated and inspired you to think a bit differently and step outside your comfort zone. Consider this book a time-sensitive call to action. Your challenge as a manager in today's workplace is to apply the most appropriate phrases and lessons in this book to your own organization's employee development process.

It's up to you, along with others on your team, to adapt and modify the phrases in this book to meet your employees' specific career development needs and objectives. It's also important to ask smart questions about the entire process as you move along.

When you ask questions, you excavate new and better ways to improve processes and move things along.

Ask yourself the following questions:

- How can I use the perfect phrases in this book to develop stronger, more effective, and timely employee development plans that will make a real difference in our organization's success and the success of its people?
- With whom will I share this information so that our organization can spread its talent development and training philosophies, while remaining consistent? Who else do I think should be reading this book?
- What examples of best practices within our organization can I capitalize on and use as models, along with the best practices models in this book, for future people development?
- How can I best demonstrate to others fast ways to use the tips, tools, and techniques in this book to update our existing employee development planning process?

Light Their Fire—Heed the Call to Action

Your genuine commitment to growing exceptional talent and creating out-of-the-box, positively outrageous employee development plans can become a legacy that you share with every employee, while helping your organization and its people to survive and thrive, inspired by a driving force of greater commitment to be better and do better.

It's time to light the fire and fire up extraordinary performance in the workplace, because America's got talent, and it literally comes to us from every corner of the world. It's our job to help plant the seeds, nurture, grow, and continue to develop it.

Here you will find the perfect phrases necessary to activate and launch a powerful employee development planning process. These phrases take all the other phrases and give them the *oomph* required to set solid career planning into motion and take career counseling efforts to a new and higher level of effectiveness.

Seven Stages of Activation

1. Turbocharge the workplace by creating an employee development environment
2. Grow talent with 21st-century technologies and forward-thinking attitudes
3. Encourage holistic development and talent building
4. Reinvent and reenergize a career—change course at any age
5. Brand talent and apply strengths
6. Add credentials to expand awareness—continuous learning and education
7. Dare to soar—grow your talent to the next level and beyond

Turbocharge the Workplace by Creating an Employee Development Environment

- Focuses on lifetime learning, not lifetime employment
- Sustains a competitive learning advantage, while learning faster than the competition
- Identifies learners' needs with assessments of real-world experience levels—asks learners, What do you need to be successful? What resources do you require to do this job?
- Understands that terms like *corporate university* and *training facility* can be misleading—physical, brick-and-mortar locations are not required for training and learning
- Seeks immediate learning opportunities anywhere in the world at any time
- Doesn't try to manage knowledge, instead evolves with it and teaches others how to apply the knowledge (The phrase *Knowledge is power* is a myth. It is not. It's what you do with the knowledge that gives you power.)
- Uses brand-name presence to leverage competitive stance in the marketplace
- Builds strategic partnerships with higher learning institutions worldwide, works in partnership with accredited universities and colleges to help employees gain higher degrees
- Combines technology with traditional classroom style training, offers the best of both worlds
- Aligns employee and talent development with the organization's critical goals

- Encourages self-directed learners who take initiative
- Offers employees access to learning resources and offers remote subject-matter experts access to help the organization learn faster
- Learns by doing
- Takes career development to a much more creative level, piques the interest of others
- Uses teach-back methods, using the organization's leadership as faculty
- Hires, trains, and promotes people to competencies
- Makes the future happen today
- No guts, no glory attitude—cannot imagine for a second *not* transitioning and evolving
- Sees a need and wants to fill it—fast
- Experiments with new career paths by volunteering first to try it out
- Starts a virtual university system for the training department
- Starts a learning lab with books, magazines, and other resources (including online resources) donated or designed by employees
- Expects everyone to brainstorm, not brain drizzle
- Defines positive expectations
- Clearly explains consequences for good and bad behaviors
- Sets up employees for success, not failure, with constant small wins built in along the way.
- Looks for buy-in, but not afraid to disagree agreeably

- Selects interdepartmental topics and includes people from those departments for discussion and input
- Leads discussions free of zingers and put-downs
- Seeks creative approaches to everything
- No whiners or martyrs allowed.
- Encourages others to put their own spin on things
- Shares all information, teaches and practices open book management (Whole Foods even shares everyone's salary!)
- Approaches all decisions with an open mind
- Deliberates but doesn't forget time restraints or deadlines
- Deadlines are sacred at times and flexible at times—knows which is which
- Focus is good.
- Fun is good.
- Takes initiative
- Takes green-light approach—sees something that needs to be done and does it, even if it's not his or her job
- Encourages creative use of position and department titles: Instead of Director of Sales and Catering, Creator of Dreams Come True; instead of Human Resources Department, People Department; instead of Product Manager, Brand Manager; instead of Chief Executive Officer, Chief of People
- Negotiates for win/win outcomes
- Takes pride in quantity and quality of work
- Meets goals and deadlines

- Exceeds goals often
- Assists others in meeting their objectives and goals
- Has a passion for achieving difficult goals
- Gives 120 percent, 100 percent of the time
- Is inspirational
- Surpasses challenging goals, helps others do the same
- Sets the bar high, then resets the bar even higher
- Loves to be the go-to person on goal setting and getting to outcomes
- Builds in flexibility and wiggle room for the unexpected that may pop up
- Annihilates challenges and what appear to be insurmountable problems
- Has will-not-stop attitude until the job is done
- Leads SWAT-like team of power players who "go for it" and make things happen
- Creates a reputation in the workplace that everyone admires
- Is confident and capable at many levels of performance and productivity, never cocky
- Understands and respects friends, extended family, and employees' home life and the balance between work and home
- Values familial responsibilities, is compassionate during hard times
- Embraces and requires cultural diversity
- Is cooperative and caring
- Is authentic, real, genuine

- Establishes core values and teaches and respects them
- Has respectful communication practices in place
- Is committed to providing cutting-edge technology, and trains and encourages employees to use it
- Has telecommuting policies in place and isn't afraid employees will be unproductive when working off-site
- Has energy in abundance
- Is friendly, makes eye contact, and smiles at people, knowing it makes them feel good
- Is fun, encourages others to lighten up, believes people live longer if they do
- Respects the environment and has green practices in place
- Is an active listener, remembers important points, recaps during conversation for clarity
- Encourages employees to be the best they can be
- Cultivates an environment of continuous learning
- Knows satisfied employees equal lower turnover
- Has fair and equitable policies
- Offers flexible work hours when possible
- Institutes maternity and paternity leave when possible
- Creates a company intranet that is accessible both on- and off-site
- Has recognition and rewards programs in place
- Creates a safe work environment, free from physical threats
- Has a tuition assistance program to encourage advanced education

- Has online and in-person employee development programs and career training opportunities available
- Breaks out of the norm of what business as usual is
- Gives year-round feedback to employees and colleagues
- Encourages, values, and rewards innovation
- Empowers staff to make decisions
- Encourages employees to better themselves through continuing education, teleseminars, webinars, and other means
- Builds morale and encourages communication among all employees
- Encourages after-hours activities, hobbies, sports, and other outside interests
- Provides stress busters on-site and encourages staff to use them during office hours when they need to blow off steam
- Encourages a fun and healthful lifestyle (Offers health fairs, an on-site gym or gym memberships, allows occasional roller-skating in hallways, etc.)
- Values and encourages creativity and provides creative outlets to foster inventive thinking
- Approaches employee education from a new direction (think Pixar University)
- Encourages collaboration and positively outrageous creativity and innovation
- Contributes to—and does not contaminate—a smart, collegial workforce
- Trusts employees, believes in their ability to do their jobs

- Understands that making mistakes is part of the learning process
- Has an eager workforce who all want to be working there
- Has a buddy/mentor program in place, knows ongoing coaching is key
- Encourages cross-training so everyone understands what everyone else does in order to further the mission of the organization
- Has employees who work toward the greater good of the organization
- Encourages networking outside the organization
- Benchmarks regularly
- Knows what people want and makes every effort to give it to them
- Makes good on promises for future development offers
- Takes the sting out of failure and helps redirect energy
- Believes in second chances
- Invents new and interesting global teleclasses, thinks Dubai, Sydney, Warsaw, here we come!

Grow Talent with 21st-Century Technologies and Forward-Thinking Attitudes

- Sees the confluence of globalization technology, environmental impact, and accommodating a multigenerational and multicultural workforce
- Fully capitalizes on all technologies
- Collaborates simultaneously online and off-line
- Creates a constantly evolving workplace
- Integrates technology and the environment to reach bottom-line goals
- Sets up boundaries without walls
- Believes in workspaces that shrink, then grow depending on the size of groups using them
- Tweaks ways to work more efficiently every day
- Enjoys rapid growth without increasing space
- Encourages telecommuting
- Drastically reduces the cost of training by using technology
- Integrates technology with traditional classroom learning
- Uses digital video conferencing tools and techniques
- Makes network security a priority
- Serves digital, high-technology consumers in a wireless workplace
- Stays on the cutting edge of international technological advances
- Likes techno gadgets, enjoys with great curiosity all the latest toys

- Encourages online social connections as an extension of powerful outreach and networking
- Reads the latest technology publications; participates in interactive forums
- Dovetails technology with functionality, giving workers a chance to learn and catch up
- Always changing and evolving the workspace
- Knows the workstation concept is where ideas are hatched
- Creates boundaries but not walls around them
- Encourages the birth of flex labs
- Motivates and stimulates teams
- Describes the training classroom of the future
- Works with both centralized and decentralized living and working issues
- Encourages new green, sustainable technology, has a can't-live-without-it attitude
- Understands how use of technology can help advance his or her career
- Uses increasing strengths of knowing technologies to grow skill sets in others
- Recognizes that unless he or she evolves and keeps up with the times, he or she will go the way of the dinosaur
- Always learns new technologies from younger or more experienced colleagues
- Understands the value of grasping technology and how that understanding can specifically help him or

her throughout an entire career to move onward and upward

- Makes technology user-friendly when possible so that everyone can be included in new learning opportunities
- Uses Skype and other webcam technologies in the workplace, looks forward to hologramming, retinal scanning, thumbprinting for fast pace, more flat-screen touch technology
- Uses IMs for the greater good
- Believes in principles of producing—not consuming—energy in the workplace
- Creates an intelligent workplace when given the opportunity using natural lighting, solar heat, Euro-sleek office furniture, ceiling panels to reflect heat, windows that actually open, wants to generate own electricity
- Combines science of workplace with creativity and innovative work styles
- Creates efficient work labs and workstations
- Turns theories into actions
- Welcomes all ideas—none are off-limits for discussion
- Sees solutions when ideas are born
- Knows great ideas can happen anywhere, at any time
- Believes it's not the size of the office, but the size of the talent pool to draw from when needed that is important

Encourage Holistic Development and Talent Building

- Investigates holistic concepts in employee development planning
- Looks for holistic talents in workers
- Sets up yoga class after work for employees
- Offers employees meditation room for quiet time
- Wants to see more organic foods in the cafeteria
- Knows that employees with balance and equilibrium do better work
- Espouses that we all must first fill people within to fill an extraordinary talent pool
- Knows self-gratification comes from workers who find meaningful purpose within the organization and within themselves
- Studies life visioning programs, applies techniques to goals and objectives
- Takes a whole-person approach to employee development
- Knows that actions come back full circle
- Realizes the most reliable "social security" is how we relate to, socialize with, and work with others
- Trusts good karma will mentor employees forward and ignite their passion
- Believes in a career mentoring philosophy with purpose
- Practices can be somewhat unorthodox when career building, but that's okay.

Reinvent and Reenergize a Career—Change Course at Any Age

- Takes risks

- Desires to manifest career and personal life goals

- Believes in leaps of faith

- Is excited to begin anew

- Helps people who have endured tough times reinvent themselves

- Uses better attitudes and forgiveness as reinvention tools

- Has no regrets, no pity parties

- Asks, "What would I do right now if I had nothing to lose and guaranteed success?"

- Asks, "What's the best that can happen if I do this?"

- Practices and encourages boundaryless thinking

- Keeps the faith under superhuman stress

- Carefully crafts life's second acts

- Says, "Don't talk about it, be about it"

- Knows the second-act theory is based on self-belief

- Believes everyone can change course if he or she wants it bad enough

- Knows age should not stand in the way of reinventing oneself

- Believes it's advisable sometimes to take a step backward in order to take a giant leap forward

- Turns "burnout" into "rock-it-out!"

- Takes stock of finances and how to "swing" self-reinvention
- Creates an energy chart to determine the time of day he or she is most "pumped up" and the time of day he or she is most tired
- Revamps his or her curriculum vitae (CV) or résumé
- Studies past successes to repeat them on a larger scale
- Finds someone who knows someone who might be doing what he or she is drawn to
- Takes a "personal board of directors" out for lunch or dinner to pick their brains for ideas
- Takes a product marketing plan off the Internet and substitutes himself or herself for the product (just Google "marketing plans")
- Focuses on the excitement of new possibilities, does not dwell on past failures
- Refuses to be frustrated
- Takes breaks, vacations, or staycations to figure out what he or she really wants
- Thinks bull's-eye! Draws a bull's-eye chart, and in the center writes his or her most desired outcomes
- Knows when to make a change before he or she burns out
- Knows when he or she jumps the shark (stops beating a dead horse and realizes when it's time to move on)
- Is not afraid to tackle new challenge with enthusiasm
- Volunteers at a nonprofit to make new contacts and friends

- Returns to school with enthusiasm
- If still in school, changes his or her major or adds a minor with confidence
- Stays active and employed even after retirement
- Has the self-awareness to know when a change is needed
- Listens to the advice of others
- Learns new skills to succeed
- Adapts to new environments
- Stretches himself or herself to reach a higher bar, likes the challenge
- Texts, Facebooks, or Skypes his or her grandkids
- Offers to take classes and self-directed steps to learn and grow
- Meets with a career counselor to identify potential opportunities
- Views career exploration like shopping—tries on a few careers for the right fit
- Thirsts for knowledge at any age

Brand Talent and Apply Strengths

- Creates his or her own signature style
- Is not afraid to exhibit a little flair in his or her personality
- Always has a contagious positive attitude
- Is approachable and friendly
- Is confident but not cocky
- Doesn't get emotional, keeps his or her cool
- Is comfortable being the "go-to" person for a given task
- Is known around the office as the expert
- Wears a smile often
- Is rational and lucid when discussing tough issues
- Speaks confidently but doesn't brag
- Is excited to share personal triumphs with colleagues (for example, shares his or her latest culinary adventure in the break room)
- Encourages others to try something new
- Inspires others
- Has hobbies that tie into work
- Has hobbies that surprise everyone
- Possesses the attitude to see projects through to completion
- Has integrity
- Has a good work ethic
- Lives the Golden Rule
- Gives and receives feedback with positive energy
- Always wants to better himself or herself

- Ignores a closed door and instead sees open windows
- Thinks creatively
- Shares his or her talents freely with others
- Learns quickly and teaches others
- Is a mentor to younger colleagues / volunteers at Big Brothers/Big Sisters
- Works well under pressure
- Is resilient
- Is always helpful
- Is upbeat
- Sees difficulties as temporary, expects to overcome them
- Does not entertain anger, loss, or discouragement for long
- Tolerates ambiguity when called for
- Is flexible, optimistic, trusting, unselfish, self-confident
- Laughs at himself or herself
- Has great sense of humor
- Accepts others as they are
- Learns lessons from all kinds of experiences
- Makes things work
- Has an independent spirit
- Is strong, durable, tough when called for
- Finds the good in the bad
- Converts misfortune into good fortune

Add Credentials to Expand Awareness— Continuous Learning and Education

- Uses lots of training assessments
- Grades himself or herself, uses self-scoring cards
- Goes on career exploration
- Uses laptop learning techniques
- Investigates all forms of funding for ongoing education
- Looks into internships
- Seeks certifications
- Investigates military resources
- Wants an apprenticeship or internship
- Targets industries for information
- Profiles industries and specific companies
- Looks into licenses and occupational agencies
- Researches President's High Growth Training Initiative (U.S. Department of Labor)
- Toys with the idea of foreign credentials, has a work visa, likes learning new languages, travelling, working, or interning overseas
- Might seek expatriate status in the United States or another country, or dual citizenship to experience international working opportunities
- Hires an international career consultant
- Encourages international studies / works and goes to school abroad
- Gets the facts to avoid online scams and fraud
- Understands accreditation and nonaccreditation

- Asks those who have the desired credentials to share their journey, contacts, and any other information available
- Sees continuing education as more than a piece of paper, but as potential to improve himself or herself
- Returns to school with gusto
- Embraces new learning opportunities
- Makes time to take classes—online or in person
- Understands that without education, he or she will become a record player in an iPod world
- Takes pride in new accomplishments
- Inspires others to seek lifelong learning, not just lifelong employment
- Seeks education when transitioning into another career

Dare to Soar—Grow Your Talent to the Next Level and Beyond

- You may be sitting in coach today, but you have first-class aspirations!

- Work your plan to be the best you can be.

- Put on your flight suit, be courageous, and take risks.

- Use your abilities to help others.

- Keep joy in your heart, and it will show outwardly.

- Don't settle for good, aspire to great!

- Treat each new day as an opportunity to do great things.

- Be confident and enthusiastic about tackling new challenges.

- Dream big, and you'll do big things.

- Take your career to new heights by keeping yourself open to learning new things.

- Be passionate about new opportunities.

- Inspire others.

- Prepare your career for takeoff.

- In the event of turbulence, seek guidance from a mentor or trusted colleague.

- In the event of an emergency, know when to evacuate.

- View roadblocks as temporary detours and mistakes as learning opportunities or chances to redirect.

- If you encounter clouds, fly above them for a clearer view.

- Always do your homework.

- If you want to be successful, make it happen!

- Success is a DIY (do-it-yourself) project.
- It's good to have your head in the game, but if you throw your heart into it, too, there's no knowing what you'll accomplish.
- Expect to do great things, and you'll do just that.
- Dress for success.
- Try to learn something new every day.
- Believe in yourself and your abilities.
- Stay curious throughout your life.
- Be considerate and thoughtful of others.
- Blaze new trails wherever you go.
- Be determined.
- You never know how or when you will make a big difference or be an inspiration to someone else.
- Never stop trying or dreaming.
- It's okay to fall down every now and again—just get back up and keep going.
- Fail forward.
- Taking the first step toward something new is often the hardest part.
- Be playful when appropriate.
- Don't be afraid to rely on others.
- Don't be intimidated.
- Observe others' spin on things.
- Listen to your higher calling, spiritual convictions, and articulate them.

Nothing Happens Until Someone Makes It Happen

The section that you just completed focuses on activating all of the previous perfect phrases lists in this book. A manager or supervisor may have all the good intentions in the world when it comes to developing his or her people and growing talent in the workplace, but without action, movement, momentum, and, ultimately, follow-through, he or she may quickly find there's not much to work with. Don't let this become your downfall as a leader. Taking an idea to a critical point and then letting it unravel is not what smart managers do.

Nothing happens until someone makes it happen. That means someone's got to design, implement, and drive the career path, employee development plan, or talent development initiative to the ultimate desired outcomes, goals, and objectives. None of this happens accidentally. These perfect phrases, and everything else in this book, come to you with both purpose and power, but it's up to you to breathe life into the phrases you select, choose how to use them in your employee planning efforts, and then demonstrate to others how to put them to work.

The conclusion to this book, which follows, will help you greatly in accomplishing this objective.

Conclusion

Talent Development Starts from the Inside Out

Employees Require Confidence to Excel

Organizations, big and small, do not crave mediocrity. The world is not hungry for people who do a so-so job. Below average doesn't cut it. Managers of successful corporations, nonprofit organizations, and government agencies know that instilling confidence in their people does not happen by focusing on employees' weaknesses and tearing down their self-esteem. Confident workers develop by maximizing and growing their unique talents and strengths. When managers focus on employees' natural talents and strengths, they build self-confidence in their people. They help employees to develop stronger self-esteem and a healthy self-image.

An employee who lacks confidence and has low self-esteem, or minimal self-worth, is like an airplane sitting out on the runway with empty fuel tanks. It may be a perfectly good airplane, but without fuel, it's not going to get off the ground and into the air, let alone reach its destination.

Remember this critical point. *Self-confidence is an employee's fuel.* Confidence is the fuel that will help your workers, and your organization, take off and soar above the clouds, just like an airplane does.

Perfect Phrases and Questions for Building Employee Confidence Levels

Here are some perfect phrases you can refer to when building employee confidence:

- You can do this.
- Here's what your career success track can look like in this organization.
- I believe in you.
- The entire team believes you can do this.
- Give yourself the benefit of the doubt.
- Let me help you build your skill set so that you can advance.
- You are worth the investment.
- Your talents are very strong.
- This seems to be your strength. How can we make sure you are doing more of this?
- What next step do you need to take to rise to the next level of your potential?
- You've demonstrated strong competencies in this area—let's add more responsibility.
- I trust you with this and want to increase your responsibilities.
- Keep asking those kinds of questions.
- You're very good at examining both sides.
- You're making wise choices and decisions—keep it up.
- The team trusts you and believes in you.

- The person who makes you angry owns you—let me help you to let go of this once and for all so that you can rise above it.

- Let's get you taking smaller risks so that you can build up to bigger risk-taking behaviors.

- What do you need to succeed? I'll do what I can to support you.

- How can I help you to feel better about yourself?

- What makes you feel insecure, and how can we avoid that from happening?

- How can I help you step outside your comfort zone?

- Whom do you depend on at work when you're in a bind?

- Let's make a list of all the things that will help build your confidence level.

- What healthy and confident behaviors would you like to practice this month?

- What makes you feel worthy?

- How can you start making better choices?

- How do you demonstrate your authenticity?

- What can you do to get past this shyness? How can I help you?

- If you had training in this area, would you feel more confident?

- Would a communication training program help you to express yourself better?

- You have what it takes to move up in the organization; let's build some self-confidence steps into your employee development plan.

- What are you afraid of? Let's face down those fears so you can move forward.
- What keeps you stuck? Let's get moving forward and leave the past behind.
- Let me help you set some realistic and attainable goals.
- Take it one step at a time and celebrate your results.
- Review your successes and start repeating them on a larger level, bit by bit.
- Give yourself credit.
- Be kind to yourself.
- It's all right, you are human.
- You can improve, don't overwhelm yourself.
- Here's something you should read.
- Have you looked at these resources?
- The team thinks you're doing a great job. Keep it up.
- We all appreciate what you've done in such a short time.
- Think of this time you are spending now as an investment in you.
- You've got what it takes.

Demonstrate to Employees Their Direct Impact on the Bottom Line

Even one employee who lacks confidence, has a poor attitude, and makes bad decisions can have a drastic impact on an organization's bottom line.

It Only Takes One

A very unmotivated baggage handler at a small Cape Cod commuter airline was unable to see the big picture of how exactly her poor decision-making skills, lack of enthusiasm for the job, and bad attitude (her manager attributed this to low self-esteem and lack of confidence) could negatively affect the entire airline and its bottom line.

Her manager pointed out to her the ripple effect she had on the company when she failed to hustle a passenger's bag to his connecting flight with only minutes to spare. The Cape Cod terminal is small, and the bag should have made it easily to the connecting flight to Martha's Vineyard. With just a bit more effort on the part of one employee, the bag could have been transferred to the connecting flight, preventing a downward spiral of customer loyalty and eventual lost revenue. What was the baggage handler's attitude? "What's in it for me if I make this extra effort? What's the rush? So what if the bag goes out on the next flight, it still gets there. It's no big deal." Wrong.

Bad Decisions Are a Big Deal

After the fact, the baggage handler's manager pointed out the impact of her actions. The valued passenger, who had an important meeting and needed his bag, which contained critical paperwork, was not pleased when he was told his bag would not arrive until the next flight, two hours later. As a result, the upset passenger shared his dismay with all the other passengers standing around at the small regional commuter's counter, and then he retold the story at his meeting. The company he worked for was the airline's biggest account, and several executives agreed not to fly this carrier again after hearing his tale.

The employee did not realize how drastically her lack of action and poor attitude could affect the business she worked for, nor did she realize that the competing carrier just down the way in Terminal B was dying to get the company's business. On top of that, the baggage handler wound up creating more work for the airline's other employees who now had to make up for her negligence.

Had specific examples of employee attitudes and the importance of self-confidence, resulting in better decision-making competencies, been detailed in an employee development plan early on, the incident might never have occurred.

Show Employees How to Reinvent and Upgrade Themselves

As more and more employees prepare for retirement, wouldn't it be nice to offer ideas to those dedicated workers on how they might reinvent themselves? We often think of succession planning as the answer to people moving on. But that's just one side of the equation. Managers often focus on who is moving into the new, vacant slot and whether he or she will be able to fill the shoes of the previous person. But what about the seasoned worker who is now leaving that spot? What does he or she do next? Shouldn't that be part of employee development planning too?

Employee development plans should be more than words on paper. Growing and nurturing talent using strategic planning methods implies movement and momentum. Managers and their employees must continue to evolve if the organization is to survive and thrive in changing times. One way to do this is by helping employees to reinvent themselves when the time is right. This happens when they manifest their career and personal life goals.

Second Acts

These are some well-known folks who have reinvented their careers in extraordinary ways:

- J. K. Rowling—from public assistance and then an English teacher to author of the Harry Potter series
- Madonna—from material girl and rock star to bestselling children's book author of *The English Roses*, and then back to being an even bigger rock star
- Al Gore—from vice president of the United States to "almost-president" to green advocate and eventually America's leader of environmentalism and Oscar winner for *An Inconvenient Truth*
- Tom Clancy—from insurance broker to bestselling novelist
- Roseanne Barr—from "domestic goddess" to superstar of her own hit TV show "Roseanne"
- Ron Howard—from playing Opie on "The Andy Griffith Show" to famous Hollywood director and Oscar winner

Sometimes Our Reinvention Is Up in the Air

In the movie *Up in the Air*, George Clooney, a modern-day traveler and corporate downsizer, offers a pivotal idea to an employee he's just terminated by suggesting the man follow his interest in and love of cooking to create a new vocation. In that single moment when Clooney connects with the human side of his business, the reality of the employee's situation, the employee's passion for cooking, and the possibility of him developing competencies that could shape an even better future all converge.

What's happening now with long-term employee development planning and succession planning is the inclusion of helping to "reinvent" the person who is moving on. Whether the person is moving on due to retirement, downsizing, early retirement opportunity, or the desire to just leave and start a new career, we owe it to the more experienced worker to help him or her create life's "second act." It's time to help workers manifest their goals and reinvent themselves through tough times and proud times.

Ron's Story: How a Technology Consultant Reboots and Reinvents a 27-Year Career

Ron's story is an example of a reinvented career. Here it is in his own words:

> "For over 27 years I have been running my technology consulting practice out of my home office. During this time my wife, Geri, was pursuing her career at Motorola. Working at home provided me with the opportunity to

get into the kitchen and at the very least begin preparation for the evening meal, which ultimately provided the luxury for two working professionals to have dinner at a reasonable hour. As time went on I found that following recipes, and in many cases altering them to my personal taste, was actually fun. The seed was planted.

"Just over two years ago, I made a promise to myself that I would attend a culinary school. The first step was to ease myself out of the day-to-day details of attending to my consulting practice. This was achieved by forming partnerships with individuals and firms that I knew and trusted. While I still maintain overall control of the engagements I am contracted with, the engineers and other consultants have absorbed the bulk of the work. Three years ago I was flying on average 130,000 miles a year. Now my annual average is about 10,000 miles.

"I had begun the process of looking into every culinary school based in the Chicago area. I identified four schools that drew my interest. Early on I eliminated one, and by the end of the first year of my analysis two schools remained as a possibility. Based on a review of curriculum and scheduling, I chose Le Cordon Bleu.

"Being old enough to apply for Social Security, I have a number of friends and associates who are just perfectly happy to sit back and do little or nothing as they wind down their careers. I don't understand that attitude. This is the time of life when you have the chance to go out and learn and/or do something new, and it is all about having fun doing it. You don't need to put yourself into the pressure cooker. This goes for typical retirees and those taking early retirement too.

"Just set your own pace. And no matter how big or small the productivity, the rewards will come. My motto: Just do it!

"Companies can greatly help employees who are moving on by offering them 'second act' advice and career planning assistance. I took the initiative and did mine on my own, but I can see the need for this in organizations everywhere."

Perfect Phrases for Employees Embarking on a "Second Act"

The other side of succession planning is not just helping the person who's stepping into a new role, but helping the person who is leaving a position with a practical step-by-step transition and a development plan that now focuses on that person's passion and life interests. It doesn't have to take a lot of time or money either. Sometimes a small change, bit of advice, or helpful encouragement is all it takes to reenergize a person's life and career. It makes life and work feel fresh again!

- Think "reboot career."
- Figure out what you want to do.
- Do you need the help of a life coach or career consultant?

- Create an "energy chart" of when you are most motivated to take on a big project.
- When are you most engaged?
- What drags you down? Stay clear of it.
- Visualize what you want.
- Start researching.
- Google your brains out.
- Investigate, call people, and ask questions.
- Join a social network that could link you to people in the profession you are looking at.
- Create a life board of directors, people whose advice you respect.
- Brainstorm with friends.
- Don't listen to the naysayers.
- Surround yourself with positive people who cheer you on.
- Is this a new business venture? If yes, how much capital will it require to get started?
- Build a nest egg to get you through the first six months.
- Build a plan to market yourself.
- Google "marketing plan."
- Revamp your résumé.
- Interview.
- Focus on an exciting future.
- Check your competencies against the opportunities.
- If it feels right, keep doing it.

Perfect Phrases Formula for Creating Lightning in a Bottle

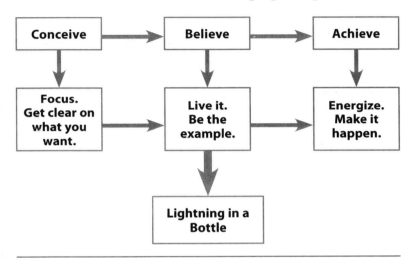

Each employee is an innovative thinker, decision maker, solution finder, problem solver, and change leader. The lightning is *within* each person. Think of each worker as the bottle—the precious container that holds talent and possibilities for a better, more productive, and joyful tomorrow. Encourage people to reinvent themselves regularly throughout their career.

Streamlining the Process

I hope that this Perfect Phrases book will help you to stream-line the process of writing employee development plans and foster continuous employee growth and development in your organization.

We all have a purpose. The real work comes in helping one another find it. And that takes a plan.

About the Author

Anne Bruce dispenses humor, wisdom, wit, and practical insights, taken from her worldwide travels and adventures, in her books, and from the speaker's platform and international seminar stage. She has built a global reputation as an impactful human behaviorist, entertaining speaker on leadership motivation, advocate for branding global talent, and bestselling author of 14 books.

Anne has had the privilege to speak, write, or train for prestigious institutions and organizations such as the White House, the Pentagon, Sony International, Best Buy, Coca-Cola, Geico, Southwest Airlines, Harvard Law School, Sprint, Ben & Jerry's, JetBlue, Baylor University Medical Center, MedAmerica Billing Services, Inc., Marriott International, the Social Security Administration, and the American Red Cross.

Her books have been translated into more than 24 languages worldwide, including career books such as *Speak for a Living: The Insider's Guide to Building a Speaking Career* (ASTD Press) and award-winning life-coaching books such as *Discover True North: A 4-Week Approach to Ignite Your Passion and Activate Your Potential* (McGraw-Hill) and *Be Your Own Mentor* (McGraw-Hill).

Anne has appeared on the "CBS Evening News" and as a guest on the "Charlie Rose Show." She's contributed interviews to NBC, MSNBC, ABC, FOX, and CNN. *USA Today*, the *Times* (London), the *Wall Street Journal*, the *San Jose Mercury News*, and *Newsweek* have interviewed Anne as well.

Anne and her husband, David, enjoy living a bicoastal beach life in both the Los Angeles area and Charleston, South Carolina. Anne is currently writing her first novel and screenplay.

For information on keynotes and training programs associated with this book and others, visit Anne's website, www.AnneBruce.com. To bring this book's training program to your organization, for information on additional leadership seminars, for fees and availability, or to schedule press interviews, call 214-507-8242 or e-mail Anne@AnneBruce.com.

The Right Phrase for Every Situation...Every Time

Perfect Phrases for Building Strong Teams
Perfect Phrases for Business Letters
Perfect Phrases for Business Proposals and Business Plans
Perfect Phrases for Business School Acceptance
Perfect Phrases for College Application Essays
Perfect Phrases for Cover Letters
Perfect Phrases for Customer Service
Perfect Phrases for Dealing with Difficult People
Perfect Phrases for Dealing with Difficult Situations at Work
Perfect Phrases for Documenting Employee Performance Problems
Perfect Phrases for Executive Presentations
Perfect Phrases for Landlords and Property Managers
Perfect Phrases for Law School Acceptance
Perfect Phrases for Lead Generation
Perfect Phrases for Managers and Supervisors
Perfect Phrases for Managing Your Small Business
Perfect Phrases for Medical School Acceptance
Perfect Phrases for Meetings
Perfect Phrases for Motivating and Rewarding Employees
Perfect Phrases for Negotiating Salary & Job Offers
Perfect Phrases for Perfect Hiring
Perfect Phrases for the Perfect Interview
Perfect Phrases for Performance Reviews
Perfect Phrases for Real Estate Agents & Brokers
Perfect Phrases for Resumes
Perfect Phrases for Sales and Marketing Copy
Perfect Phrases for the Sales Call
Perfect Phrases for Sales Presentations
Perfect Phrases for Setting Performance Goals
Perfect Phrases for Small Business Owners
Perfect Phrases for the TOEFL Speaking and Writing Sections
Perfect Phrases for Writing Company Announcements
Perfect Phrases for Writing Grant Proposals
Perfect Phrases in American Sign Language for Beginners
Perfect Phrases in French for Confident Travel
Perfect Phrases in German for Confident Travel
Perfect Phrases in Italian for Confident Travel
Perfect Phrases in Spanish for Confident Travel to Mexico
Perfect Phrases in Spanish for Construction
Perfect Phrases in Spanish for Gardening and Landscaping

Visit mhprofessional.com/perfectphrases for a complete product listing.

Learn more. Mc Graw Hill Do more.

3 1985 00221 2798